"Grounded in deep insights, this book is a practical guide to marketing to Generation Z. With Jeff's relentless pursuit of uncovering relevant and timely insights, you'll find actionable strategies to motivate this powerful Gen Z consumer to buy."

—STEPHANIE WISSINK, Managing Director,
Consumer Research, Jefferies LLC

"With Gen Z poised to comprise 40 percent of consumers by 2020, brand leaders don't have time to waste when it comes to developing a full understanding of what the authors have endearingly tagged as 'Pivotals.' Jeff and Angie have painted a rich picture of the youngest generation in the marketplace; a portrait replete with behavioral and attitudinal observations that help the marketer draw sharp distinctions between Pivotals and the generations that precede them."

—DON FOX, Chief Executive Officer,
Firehouse of America LLC

"An easy-to-read, go-to playbook for anyone trying to better understand and market directly to Gen Z. Rooted in solid research, *Marketing to Gen Z* provides colorful real-world brand examples and actionable insights for marketers hoping to win with young consumers."

—JON GRANT, Associate Director, Product
Marketing, Square Enix

"*Marketing to Gen Z* is a comprehensive analysis of sound research and case studies that provides brands with a roadmap to reaching what is a distinctive, second 'Greatest Generation.'"

—MARY MCILRATH, Ph.D., C+R
Research/YouthBeat

"Angie Read and Jeff Fromm paint a thoughtful, practical portrait of my daughters' generation in *Marketing to Gen Z*. One that has me hoping they're proud of what we've built but certainly confident of how they'll improve the financial wellbeing of our society."

—CHRIS COSTELLO, CEO, blooom

"As someone who has been doing this a long time, I was forced to admit I knew even less than I thought I did about Gen Z. Start to finish, *Marketing to Gen Z* is filled with unexpected attributes and keen insights—backed by data and real-life stories—about this surprising generation. I'm not only better educated and prepared to market to Gen Z, I'm also generally more optimistic about the future, knowing who's going to be in charge in a few years!"

—LAURIE ELLISON, Chief Marketing
Officer, Children's Hospital

"The breadth of insights and perspective shared provide an invaluable guidebook for marketers to ensure they remain relevant and understand how to connect with Gen Z—aka 'Pivotals'—and their evolving influence. They are savvy marketers of brand 'me,' so strategies and messaging need to be authentic, real and relatable. It's time to stop selling and start supporting a greater purpose."

—MARLA KAPLOWITZ, President-CEO, 4A's (American
Association of Advertising Agencies)

"The next generation of explorers will value unique, customized digital and physical experiences. This book provides valuable clues to market and communicate with them on their terms."

—JILL CRESS, Chief Marketing Officer,
National Geographic

"Gen Z is financially savvy and savings-minded. *Marketing to Gen Z* should be considered essential reading for brands—and others—trying to understand this new generation of consumers."

—JILL COLE, Chief Marketing Officer, Thrivent
Education Finance Group

MARKETING TO
GENZ

MARKETING TO

GENZ

THE RULES FOR REACHING THIS VAST
AND VERY DIFFERENT
GENERATION OF INFLUENCERS

JEFF FROMM / ANGIE READ

AMACOM
AMERICAN MANAGEMENT ASSOCIATION
New York • Atlanta • Brussels • Chicago • Mexico City • San Francisco
Shanghai • Tokyo • Toronto • Washington, D.C.

Bulk discounts available. For details visit:
www.amacombooks.org/go/specialsales
Or contact special sales:
Phone: 800-250-5308
E-mail: specialsls@amanet.org
View all the AMACOM titles at: www.amacombooks.org
American Management Association: www.amanet.org

This publication is designed to provide accurate and authoritative information in regard to the subject matter covered. It is sold with the understanding that the publisher is not engaged in rendering legal, accounting, or other professional service. If legal advice or other expert assistance is required, the services of a competent professional person should be sought.

Library of Congress Cataloging-in-Publication Data

Names: Fromm, Jeff, author. | Read, Angie.
Title: Marketing to Gen Z : the rules for reaching this vast--and very
    different--generation of influencers / Jeff Fromm and Angie Read.
Description: New York : AMACOM, [2018] | Includes index.
Identifiers: LCCN 2017038847 (print) | LCCN 2017047235 (ebook) | ISBN
    9780814439289 (ebook) | ISBN 9780814439272 (hardcover)
Subjects: LCSH: Young adult consumers--Attitudes. | Target marketing. |
    Consumer behavior.
Classification: LCC HF5415.332.Y66 (ebook) | LCC HF5415.332.Y66 F758 2018
    (print) | DDC 658.8/340842--dc23
LC record available at https://lccn.loc.gov/2017038847

About AMA
American Management Association (www.amanet.org) is a world leader in talent development, advancing the skills of individuals to drive business success. Our mission is to support the goals of individuals and organizations through a complete range of products and services, including classroom and virtual seminars, webcasts, webinars, podcasts, conferences, corporate and government solutions, business books, and research. AMA's approach to improving performance combines experiential learning—learning through doing—with opportunities for ongoing professional growth at every step of one's career journey.

10 9 8 7 6 5 4 3 2 1

CONTENTS

ACKNOWLEDGMENTS

A project like this takes a village. And we had a great and active group of villagers from the early days of conceiving this work.

This project first took shape with the teams at Barkley and Future-Cast creating and publishing a massive consumer research study called "Getting to Know Gen Z" that included secondary analysis across a broad range of sources, followed by both qualitative and quantitative consumer studies. We completed this research work to ensure we had the deepest possible view of Gen Z. For the efforts of all our partners, we say thank you to Joe Cardador, Ph.D., Tim Galles, David Gutting, Brad Hanna, Shelby Haydon, Skyler Huff, Chad Nicholson, Jason Parks, Brendan Shaughnessy, Leah Swartz, Greg Vodicka, Meg Zych, and many others who chipped in to make this a full 360-degree view of these emerging consumers, as well as their distinct differences from prior generations.

Next, we would also like to thank Sarah Crawford, our talented and tenacious senior editor; Ilana Bodker, our thoughtful, witty junior editor; Art Ramirez, our amazing designer; Kelly Thompson, our project manager; Joanne B. Jarvi, our agent; Lisa Chase, Amy Allen, Rio Cervantes-Reed, as well as Ellen Kadin and her team at AMA-COM. We also had a number of experts who read drafts of the book, providing valuable clues on gaps that needed to be filled before we turned the book over to the publisher. We'd like to acknowledge each of them with a big thank-you: Chase Wagner, Nick Bartlow, Chad

Nicholson, Joe Cardador, PhD., Jenny Thayer, David Gutting, Peri Shaplow, Elisa Schauer, Anne Lamberti, and Josh Burch.

Finally, we have some individual thoughts to share.

From Angie: To say the past year has been a daunting yet exciting journey would be a huge understatement. I took a leap of faith to follow my passion for and commitment to evangelizing Gen Z, and it turned into a once-in-a-lifetime opportunity to work with Jeff Fromm, FutureCast, and Barkley to write this book. I couldn't be more grateful to Jeff for believing in me and asking me to partner with him on this book. It's already been a wild ride, and I look forward to seeing where we go from here! Your support and mentorship mean the world to me.

I have many friends and family members to acknowledge as well. Thank you, Brent Bowen, for planting a seed with five little words: "You should write a book." Remember how I thought you were crazy at the time? Thank you, Mom, Linda Hall, for watering that seed, and for being my first reader and biggest cheerleader. Thank you, Steve Doyal, my protective and supportive husband, for never doubting me or allowing me to doubt myself. And to my favorite Gen Zers on the planet—Sammy, Henry, and Gabby Gutierrez—I couldn't be more proud to be your mom. You inspire and amaze me every day in your awesome "Z-ness."

Finally, thank you, Steve Hall, Ken and Lissa Read, Pam and Dion Reihs, Melissa and Doug Jackson, Chris and Becca Hodges, Jared Doyal, Trevor Doyal, Mike Engsberg, Hollie Carrender-Shephard, Stephanie Kelly, Kristin Ford, Josh Richardson, the No Coast Riders (NCR), and the rest of my amazing tribe for always believing in me.

From Jeff: This was my first experience authoring a book on a generation other than Millennials, and it could not have been a more fulfilling experience. Angie was a wonderful and spirited leader when it came to writing the book. She truly captured and codified what we hoped to share with each of you about this fascinating, up-and-coming Gen Z.

Thank you to my incredible family—my wife, Rhonda, and my children, Laura, Abby, and Scott. Additional thank-yous to Bill Fromm, Bernie Fromm, Jackie Fromm, Andy Fromm, Dan Fromm, Marti Fromm, Eddie Fromm, and Julie Fromm for all of their support. Without all of you, none of this would be possible.

With our sincerest thanks,
Angie and Jeff

FOREWORD

Some brands may disregard Gen Z as too young or too insignificant, but as CEO of Dairy Queen, I've already seen the impact this youthful audience holds. This cohort of teenagers influences the market financially, culturally, technologically, and economically—and this influence will only continue to grow.

At Dairy Queen, we don't have customers, we have fans. As a seventy-seven-year-old brand, it is vital that we understand and create an emotional bond with our fans of the future. Often, this requires adjusting our brand strategy, product offerings, and marketing outreach to appeal to younger generations like the Zs. For companies to successfully adapt, it is vital to understand who the Gen Zs are, how they interact with brands, and, in our case, how to make them raving fans of the DQ brand for life.

We were once told that we needed to pay attention because Millennials were the future, and this was true. Now, as Millennials become parents, and Gen Z takes their place, this next generation's participation will once again be the key to success for many of today's brands, including my own.

Yet, it's not as simple as applying the same tactics we learned for the Millennial generation.

As you'll find out in the first few pages of this book, the characteristics of Gen Z are entirely different from those of Millennials. They are the young pragmatists that Millennials were not, surrounded by mobile technology since leaving the womb. They grew up in a post-

9/11 world. Witnessing the election of the first black president and the Great Recession were the defining moments of their youth. They are multitaskers, progressives, and purposeful souls, already aware of their capabilities and the power they can achieve.

You might see them out with their families, typing furiously on their mobile phones. Maybe you see them walking out of school, on the way to their part-time jobs or extracurricular activities. You may see them at a concert, dancing and filming videos for their Snapchat stories. This generation is made of expression, dedication, shrewdness, and hard work. And these young people aren't just the future; they are the present.

With its explanations of Gen Z's values, upbringing, and beliefs, this book truly generates an appreciation for a group that was, and still very much is, an enigma for marketers. *Marketing to Gen Z* utilizes this information to delve into the nuances of reaching them: Seamless video content that manages to be authentic, personable, and secure. Leveraging Gen Z's constant self-curation to have your brand mutually support theirs. Making in-store shopping an experience in and of itself. These are all tactics—but hardly an exhaustive list—researched and detailed by Barkley and FutureCast within this book, making it the most useful resource to every marketer seeking a leg-up on the generation poised to change the entirety of the market—and the world.

—John Gainor, President and CEO of Dairy Queen

INTRODUCTION

Kate Jackson, a 17-year-old from Kansas City, Missouri, is just finishing her shift as a dishwasher and busser at Heirloom Bakery and Hearth. As usual, Kate is in a bit of a rush to get home to finish her homework, so she stops at one of her favorite restaurants, Chipotle, to grab a burrito bowl before heading home to hit the books.

Kate is a senior at Lincoln College Prep Academy, but tomorrow morning she'll head to Penn Valley Community College, where she's enrolled in its early college prep program. When she graduates from Lincoln Prep next spring (with honors), she will have earned both a high school diploma *and* an associate's degree. She'll also have about 60 college credits, which means she'll automatically be a junior in college. She's excited about all the money she'll save on college tuition!

Today, Kate wants to major in chemistry, because "it will give me plenty of career options." But Kate's real desire is to be a crime scene investigator, so she can see herself pursuing a master's degree in forensic science—but not before she studies abroad. Kate's family has hosted five foreign exchange students in the past decade, so she is anxious to experience other cultures.

Between classes tomorrow, Kate will hang out with her diverse group of friends, including her boyfriend, Jose, a Mexican immigrant; Blair, a white bisexual; and Sharon, who is black and identifies as gender nonbinary (as does Jose). They may discuss the latest play they're all in, the top news story of the day, or maybe a funny YouTube video.

In the evening, Kate will go home to hang out with her family, play *Dungeons and Dragons*, or perhaps read (she proudly self-identifies as a bookworm). Whatever she ends up doing, Kate probably won't advertise it on social media as the rest of her friends do, as she's a little less social than they are. She's just as happy hanging out by herself as shopping with her friends at Forever 21 (Kate loves their $10-and-under section). She also loves to spend time volunteering at the local animal shelter. But these days, free time is hard to come by. Kate is laser-focused on keeping her grades up, earning money for college, and planning for her future.

Kate and her group of friends are quintessential Gen Z.

Great. Just when we thought we had Millennials figured out, a new generation of young consumers forces us into uncharted territory yet again.

While new to the scene, Kate and her Gen Z friends are not mysterious or even elusive. What they are, however, is resolute. Smart. Pragmatic. Hardworking. Entrepreneurial.

But are we really surprised? After all, each new generation brings its own set of attitudes, beliefs, and behaviors, and Generation Z is simply responding to an environment shaped by economic instability and social change. It's our job, as marketers, to adapt and adjust to these changes. Which isn't easy, as we've learned from our decade-long challenge of marketing to Millennials.

Reaching Generation Z will be just as demanding, if not more so, but it may also be the most enlightening and rewarding adventure of our careers. Kate represents an exciting generation destined to change the world.

And change the world they will. Gen Z is on track to become the largest generation, expected to represent 40 percent of consumers by the year 2020.[1] They represent approximately $44 billion in direct buying power.[2] And after you factor in their unprecedented influence on family spending (93 percent of parents say their children influence family and household purchases, Deep Focus's Cassandra Report, 2015), that number jumps considerably. If you look at what parents and caregivers spend on Gen Z, they wield influence over as much as $255 billion. Taking it a step further, if you look at total household expenditures, the potential for Gen Z's impact on other spending may be more than $665 billion.[3] Generation Z is large, powerful, and challenging. Just as Kate sets high standards for herself, Gen Z expects brands to strive for excellence. These teens are powerful, passionate, and ready to engage.

In the postdigital, consumer-controlled economy of today, marketing to this group won't be easy. In fact, many organizations are still totally preoccupied with the Millennial generation; they've overlooked the potential of Generation Z.

But we can't really judge them; we've been rather preoccupied ourselves. Millennials were our original muse. We study them diligently at FutureCast, a marketing consultancy specializing in modern consumer trends. We literally wrote the book on Millennials.

Two, actually: *Marketing to Millennials* (2013) and *Millennials with Kids* (2015).

And in our research we began to recognize the major influences of Gen Z. We were fascinated and wanted to learn more. The same curiosity that fuels our investigation of the Millennial generation prompted us to add Gen Z exploration to our agenda.

As a result, we conducted one of the first deep-dive research projects with our partner and parent company, Barkley, to better understand the behaviors, attitudes, and motivations of Generation Z.

METHODOLOGY

The key questions that served as the cornerstone of our research included:

1. How is Gen Z different from the Millennial generation?
2. What does Gen Z believe and value?
3. What perspectives shape their experiences?
4. When faced with decisions, what drives Gen Z to make a choice?
5. What makes brands relevant to Gen Z?

Our primary piece of research was a quantitative, cross-generational, nationally representative study fielded in September 2016. We explored purchase and spending behaviors, attitudes, beliefs, and motivations across all generations (Gen Z = age 15–19, Millennials = 20–35, Gen X = 36–51, Boomers = 52–70; total sample size 2,039, of which 505 were Gen Zs) as they related to:

▶ Views on self (health/wellness/nutrition), society (workers/ wages/cause), planet (environment/sustainability), and the role of brands
▶ Brand expectations
▶ Media habits
▶ Shopping habits (retail and restaurant segments and channels)
▶ Information access

In addition to quantitative research, we spent a month working and shopping with teens to gain better insight into how they spend their time on a daily basis and what motivates them on a personal level.

So what did we learn? The answers may surprise you.

Battling the duality of traditional and nonconformist values, Gen Z challenges us to move the world forward. Earnest, hardworking, and driven by conservative views of success regarding money, education, and career advancement, Gen Zers resemble a much older generation.

But their personal beliefs tell a different story. This generation is writing modern rules that favor liberal views on race, gender, identity, and sexuality. Socially and technologically empowered, Generation Z arrives on the scene at a crucial moment in history. While Millennials dreamed of changing the world, Gen Z is wide awake and poised to actually make the moves.

In the following chapters, we will delve into the forces shaping Gen Z, as well as the statistics at play. We'll investigate the rules governing

TRADITIONAL	NONCONFORMIST
Conservative behaviors	Liberal views
Focus on personal success	Driven by power in numbers and group acceptance
Interest in branded material goods	Desire to not conform to traditional notions of sexual preference
Considers having a family a high priority	Does not conform to traditional notions of sexual preference
Values education	Entrepreneurial and skill oriented
Financially savvy and aware	Thinks globally, not just locally

Figure I-1 Generation Z's traditional versus nonconformist duality.[1]

their social media use and how, at a very young age, many Gen Zers build a personal brand.

From there, we'll take a look at how brands today succeed with Gen Z and where they find inspiration. We'll explore the evolution of social media and marketing, our predictions for this generation, and the future of the market in their hands.

And to ensure you start off on the right foot with this up-and-coming generation, we compiled chapters rich in tactics that are ideal for reaching emergent consumers because, while some Gen Zers are still in middle school, marketing to this generation isn't child's play. Teens today represent one of the most powerful consumer forces in the world; as they form their own brand preferences and develop personal buying behaviors, businesses must adapt to meet their expectations.

It's taken us years to capture and engage Millennial consumers, and many marketers aren't ready for yet another shift. There's no denying that Gen Z challenges our methods and strategy; these divergent youths command the support of their ambition. Brands that work to understand *and* follow their rules will reap the rewards, and those that don't will quickly be ignored. And that's a best-case scenario.

WHO IS GEN Z?

Nobody can agree on exactly when the Millennial generation stops and Gen Z starts. Demographers generally say the first Gen Zers were born in the early to mid-1990s through the mid-2000s. For the sake of this book, based on our research, we're using birth years 1996 to 2010 as our parameters.

Speaking of birth years, we've developed a general timeline of modern generations (birth year ranges vary, depending on source). As we discuss commonalities and differences between Gen Z and other generations, this will serve as a handy reference:

- ► Silent Generation: 1925–1945
- ► Boomers: 1946–1964
- ► Gen X: 1965–1978
- ► Millennials (sometimes called Gen Y): 1979–1995
- ► Gen Z: 1996–2010

A GENERATION DEFINED BY CHANGE

Besides birth years, generations are defined by other factors, including the most impactful moments of their early lives. Generations develop strong emotional connections to these formative experiences, which impact how they view themselves and the world around them.

For example, while some were alive on 9/11, most Gen Zers can't recall the tragedy. For Millennials, however, the terror and destruction of the event left a definitive mark in their memory. For them, emotional conversations spring up at the mention of the day, many recalling where they were, what they were doing, and how they felt when the first plane hit. For some, this is one of their earliest memories of fear. The news reports and precautions against terror alerted their developing minds to the harsh realities of a broken world.

For Gen Z, progress, not fear, is spurring this generation into action. As Barack Obama was sworn into office as the first black president of the United States of America, Generation Z watched in wonder and internalized a deep sense of progress. The battle cry for racial equality reached a climax that day—and again following his reelection—with Gen Z stepping up to carry the torch.

Let's look at a breakdown of the generations again, only this time showcasing a few of their most defining moments. (See Figure 1-1.)

Based on similarities in their defining moments and how these moments subsequently shaped their view of the world, some say Gen Z has more in common with the Silent Generation and Boomers than with Millennials. Whereas Millennials evince a story of "innocence lost," Gen Z has never known a world without war and the threat of domestic terrorism. Like their grandparents and great-grandparents who grew up in the wake of World War II and the Great Depression, Gen Z is growing up in a post-9/11 world marked by the Great Recession.

While many describe Gen Z as "Millennials on steroids," we not only disagree but will illustrate clear proof otherwise.

Figure 1-1   The events that define a generation.

In fact, based on what we learned in our 2017 research study with Barkley, "Getting to Know Gen Z: How the Pivotal Generation Is Different from Millennials," we think the most fitting term for members of this generation is **"Pivotals."** They are pivoting away from common Millennial behaviors and attitudes and veering toward a socially conscious and diverse era reminiscent of the no-nonsense consumers of yesteryear.

THE FIRST POST-RACE GENERATION

I'm confident that Gen Z, having grown up at a time when social norms have changed dramatically, will be the first post-race, post-gender generation.

—**GRACE MASBACK, 18,** *THE VOICE OF GEN Z: UNDERSTANDING THE ATTITUDES & ATTRIBUTES OF AMERICA'S NEXT "GREATEST GENERATION"*

Every generation makes its own strides. Whether it's civil liberties, technological advances, environmentalism, or artistic revivals, each decade brings about a new era. But the Pivotal Generation, over-achievers that they are, accomplished a progressive goal hundreds of years in the making.

Grace Masback is a Pivotal and activist who wrote a book on the social consciousness of her generation. In her book *The Voice of Gen Z: Understanding the Attitudes & Attributes of America's Next "Greatest Generation,"* Grace passionately promotes the values of her peer group. She believes that, "although we certainly 'see' race, we have grown up in a world where anyone and everyone can be our friend."

Powered by her writing talent and passion for political activism, Grace represents just one of many Pivotal individuals who takes pride in diversity and inclusivity. The origin of this ethnic embrace? The steady decline of the white majority.

Pivotals will be the last white-majority generation. To help put this in perspective, since the early 1700s, the most common last names in the United States have been Smith, Johnson, and Williams. Today, Garcia, Martinez, and Rodriguez are inching closer to the top.[1]

Let's take a closer look:

- ▶ Fifty-five percent of Pivotals are white, 24 percent are Hispanic, 14 percent are African American, and 4 percent percent are Asian. On the other hand, 70 percent of Boomers are white.[2] (See Figure 1-2.)
- ▶ In 2013, 10 percent of births were multiracial. This is a stark contrast from 1970, when only 1 percent of births yielded a child of more than one race.[3] (See Figure 1-3.)
- ▶ In the last 30 years, we have seen a 400 percent increase in multiracial marriages (with a 1,000 percent increase in Asian–white marriages).[4]

PIVOTALS   BOOMERS

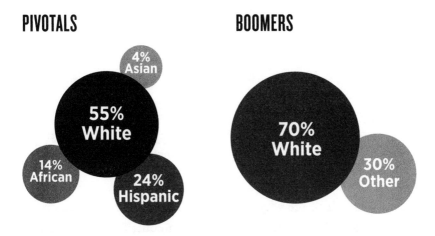

Figure 1-2   Race of Boomers versus Pivotals.

Figure 1-3   Multiracial births in 1970 versus 2013.

▶ There also has been a 134 percent increase of people who self-identify as mixed white-and-black biracial and an 87 percent increase of mixed white-and-Asian descent.[5]

Considering these stats, it is no surprise that Pivotals are ready to fight the battle for diversity and multiculturalism. They possess a racial wisdom far beyond their years.

"WE'RE NOT WHO YOU THINK WE ARE"

I was raised in a household where I was taught to ask myself *"how* am I going to make a difference?" not *"if* I am going to make a difference." I am a product of my environment, committed to change-making.

—ZIAD AHMED, 18, FOUNDER AND PRESIDENT OF REDEFY AND CO-FOUNDER OF JÜV CONSULTING

It's not difficult to see why President Obama, among others, recognized this 18-year-old for his passion and contributions to further equality. Ziad is the founder and president of Redefy, a youth organization created to challenge prejudice and sexism. He also cofounded Jüv Consulting to give teenage consultants a voice in the business world.

Typical myths surrounding the young are that they're restless and reckless. You know, like, "Kids these days . . . they're out of control!"

But Pivotals are hardworking, financially responsible, independent, and determined—characteristics not usually assigned to teenagers. They also are less likely than previous generations to engage in risky behaviors like underage drinking, drugs, or smoking. Because they tend to exhibit more conservative behaviors, it's understandable that they also maintain more traditional attitudes regarding honesty, loyalty, and achievement.

It is important to note that, while the pendulum may swing backward in some ways, the world we live in today differs from the one that existed 50 years ago. While we continue to see teens follow a more traditional path, we cannot expect the exact behavior of their elders. Like Millennials, Pivotals operate in a market guided by technological advancements and a social landscape spanning the physical and digital worlds.

NOT MILLENNIALS ON STEROIDS

The biggest mistake [brands are making when marketing to Gen Z] is thinking we're exactly like Millennials. They need to ask "What are the differences?" We know everything is earned. Nothing is given.

—CONNOR BLAKLEY, 18, FOUNDER OF YOUTHLOGIC AND AUTHOR OF *BRANDZ*

Of course, not comparing the two generations is easier said than done, considering the decade-long and continuing effort to understand and market to Millennials. It's impossible to differentiate the generations without making some side-by-side comparisons.

So, let's dig in.

Some of the most obvious similarities include both generations' familiarity with technology and expectations for 24/7 digital access. They share a love of social media, extensive friend networks, and visibility into the lives of others. They both desire active participation and cocreation with brands, and pledge to make a difference in the world.

But don't let the similarities mislead you. Treating Pivotals like younger Millennials—rather than approaching them as a separate consumer group with their own views, ideas, need states, and expectations of brands—is a huge mistake, one that they do not take lightly.

Let's do a quick side-by-side comparison of Pivotals to Millennials. For instance, Pivotals can multitask across five screens at once (TV, phone, laptop, desktop, and either a tablet or handheld gaming device), while Millennials typically stick to maneuvering two screens simultaneously (TV and phone, or phone and laptop, etc.).

Thanks to the continued uptick in technological advancements, Pivotals think in 4D versus 3D. They have grown up with hi-def, surround

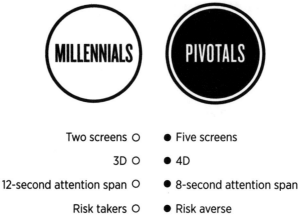

Figure 1-4 Millennials versus Pivotals.

sound, and now 360-degree photography and film (i.e., virtual reality). Even with so many entertainment luxuries, Pivotals are more realistic about things like jobs and finances than Millennials, as a result of having grown up in a time of great turmoil. (See Figure 1-4.)

THE DESIRES THAT DRIVE

People say they don't see color, but everyone sees color. There's not a problem with seeing color. There's a problem with how you treat people based on their color and ethnic background. You're allowed to recognize that people are from different cultures and that's cool, it's just more about being open to other people's cultures. The more we do that, the better things will be.

—CHLOE A., 18

Pivotals want to change the world, and if we're placing bets, our money's on them to do it.

Everything we see and experience growing up—music, food, fashion, family, cultural values—shapes our generation. The same goes for Pivotals. The list of influences driving the Pivotal mind, aka the motivation behind what makes them tick, isn't short. However, to understand this generation, a broad overview is key.

PIVOTALS WERE RAISED ON. . .

Technology

Teenagers today still go through puberty, adolescence, and all the associated personal and relational dramas that go along with that. But we need to acknowledge that the technology they have grown up with has completely changed the way people go about their lives.

—CHRIS HUDSON, "HOW GENERATION Z ARE BEING SHAPED BY TECHNOLOGY"[6]

Today's teens are the first generation of consumers to have grown up in an entirely postdigital era. Pivotals have never known a world without smartphones and social media. To them, it's just the way the world works—a normal part of their daily lives. For those who classify Millennials in this category, authors Thomas Koulopoulos and Dan Keldsen in of *The Gen Z Effect*, clarify: "We view Millennials as beta testers for the true digital natives of Gen Z."

To connect with Pivotals, technology should be invisible. User experiences should be seamless. Speeds should be fast—preferably imperceptible. And, of course, everything needs to work flawlessly on mobile. If Pivotals notice the technology, you're doing something wrong.

Multi-Tasking

Gen Z can quickly and efficiently shift between work and play, with multiple distractions going on in the background . . . working on multiple tasks at once. Talk about multi-multi-tasking.

—GEORGE BEALL, "8 KEY DIFFERENCES BETWEEN
GEN Z AND MILLENNIALS"[7]

Pivotals sometimes get a bad rap for having the attention span of goldfish. But it's not that they lack focus—their brains are actually adapting to their digital environment faster than the brains of previous generations. They are used to having massive amounts of information thrown at them at lightning speed, so they have become used to processing it just as quickly.

Pivotals have the ability to filter out content within an eight-second window (or less) and can decide very quickly what brings value or interests them.

Short attention spans aside, talk to the parent of any teenager, and you'll hear tales of mind-blowing multitasking skills. Writing a book report on their laptop while playing online video games with one group of friends and FaceTiming *another* group of friends—they are masters at moving between tasks with ease.

Intelligence

Go ahead, call them nerds. They don't care. In fact, it's a badge of honor. Pivotals pride themselves on their intelligence, work ethic, and creativity. According to a study conducted by Adobe, 56 percent of Pivotal students have a dream job in mind, and 88 percent plan on attending college.[8] These goals point to students who not only possess the capacity to dream of a future but the grit to do the work.

The drive to succeed doesn't stop when the bell rings. Per a recent Cassandra Report, 89 percent of Pivotals spend their free time engaging in productive activities instead of merely hanging out.[9] Among Pivotals, in the 2015 Nielsen survey "Global Generational Lifestyles: How We Live, Eat, Play, Work and Save for Our Futures," more respondents selected reading as an activity favored over watching TV.

And check out *what* they're reading. *Teen Vogue*'s December 2016 op-ed piece "Donald Trump Is Gaslighting America" caught the attention of Twitter and mainstream media.[10] Teen girl magazines certainly didn't cover such deep and controversial political topics 10 years ago. Not only are important national (and international) issues top-of-mind for today's teens, but they want to discuss these issues and make their voices heard.

So, smart? Yes. But also more mature than teens of yesteryear. Some say that's because they've been forced to grow up too fast. Whether that's due to the reality of the world we live in today, parents who want to prepare their kids for the "real world," or the media—or a combination of the three—being a kid and teenager today is a tougher business.

Social Media

Around 2010 (when the oldest Pivotal was about 14 years old), social media became mainstream, and subsequently so did the platforms Pinterest, Instagram, and Snapchat. Close to the same time, Facebook and Twitter (already considered seniors in the space) hit one billion and 500 million users, respectively. Teens today truly can't recall a life without social media.

As such, Pivotals lead when it comes to usage of traditional social media platforms, if such a term applies. However, we see a shift in social media usage away from the oversharing Millennial mentality to the current mentality of broadcasting only *specific* stories to *spe-*

cific people on *specific* channels. When we look at teens' most used platforms, it's evident Pivotals prefer selective broadcasting rather than broadly sharing the minutiae of their lives. (See Figure 1-5.)

Perceptive and savvy, Pivotals learned from the mistakes of the previous generation and are much more careful about what and where they post online. However, they don't want to walk on eggshells. They're still looking for ways to let their hair down and show their "unfiltered" selves—but they're smart enough to limit anything potentially questionable to a small circle of friends in specific social platforms.

Brands must tread lightly when trying to reach Pivotals on social media. Unless a brand knows its editorial authority—what it has permission to talk about based on the true beliefs of the brand—it won't resonate with this consumer group. Brands should avoid "marketing" in social media and instead focus on conversations.

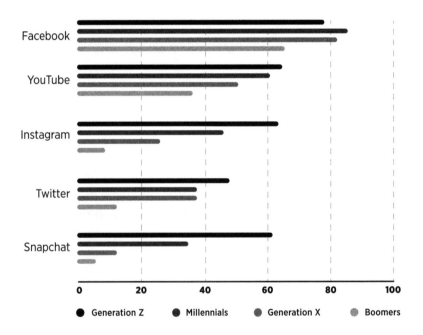

Figure 1-5 Social media usage by generation.[11]

If you try to sell, you will fail.

The best approach is to listen to Pivotals and then engage in an authentic, meaningful way. More on this in Chapter 2.

Caution

Growing up in an uncertain world, Pivotals crave safety. In a recent *Forbes* article, author Ryan Scott said they are more cautious than Gen X and Millennials were as teens, steering away from risky behaviors and toward more sensible careers and choices. Also, they're getting into less trouble than teens of previous generations. Underage drinking is on the decline, and always wearing seatbelts is a no-brainer.[12] Teen births have also declined, according to the Annie E. Casey Foundation's 2016 KIDS COUNT Data Book.[13]

And as previously mentioned, unlike Millennials, Pivotals are less interested in sharing their lives for the entire world to see. They much prefer not to leave a permanent record with ephemeral social media platforms like Snapchat.

PIVOTALS WORRY ABOUT. . .

Terrorism and Violence

Terrorism has impacted my generation in ways almost unexplainable. With 9/11, Columbine, and ISIS, Gen Z is very conscious and security-minded, but also have a desire to change the world because of this: we see things and want to change them. We've never known a world without widespread terror.

—JENN LITTLE, "GENERATION Z: WHO WE ARE."[14]

Most of us can remember the pre-9/11 days of lax airport security, when schools, movie theaters, and music concerts felt safe. Unfortunately, Pivotals have hardly known a world free from random violence. Tragedies like the Manchester bombing, the Boston Marathon attack, and the Orlando nightclub shooting deeply upset Pivotals, but sadly, they are not surprised by them.

Perhaps that's why terror and violence are the top concerns of the world's youth. Varkey Foundation, a group dedicated to global education, conducted a survey to measure the impact of terror on this generation. According to their findings, 82 percent of young Americans find the rise in violence and terror a serious, if not a dire concern.[15]

Pivotals are a serious bunch who know the world is an imperfect, scary place. One of the biggest mistakes a brand can make is portraying idealistic or fake narratives in their marketing that say otherwise. Pivotals are realistic and expect authentic stories shared by real people, content more in line with their day-to-day life. No longer do our teens want content designed for the unattainable ideal. They demand advertising serve as a reflection of their lifestyle, not a crystal ball of what could be.

The Economy

The biggest financial event of Pivotals' lifetime (so far) has been the Great Recession, which is widely considered the worst global economic downturn since World War II. They might be too young to remember specifics, but they've lived in the aftermath of the recession for most of their lives.

However, there is a silver lining. Life coach and author Christine Hassler says, "Growing up in an uncertain economy and being raised by more frugal and skeptical Gen Xers has shaped a less entitled, more money-conscious generational cohort."[16]

Financial stability is important to Pivotals, and they aren't waiting to do something about it. The Lincoln Financial Group says that the average age of opening a savings account is now 13.[17] Thirteen! Not only are these teens saving for college, as you would expect, but they also are prioritizing finding well-paying jobs and planning for retirement someday. Many are seeking formal training in financial planning; high schools and colleges are responding by offering financial-planning courses.

Understanding that great paying jobs aren't just handed out with diplomas, most college students are also focused on finding jobs that offer financial security, such as those in science, technology, engineering, and math (STEM), even if that means putting one's passion on the back burner. This is in stark contrast with the Millennial mindset of chasing their passion and finding that "dream job." Regarding career concerns, *Fast Company* reports a penchant for financial stability among Pivotals. "They're obsessed with developing contingency plans to help them navigate the dynamic job market."[18]

I try to save as much as I can because I learned in personal finance class that the interest from savings would increase in value and you can have a lot of money if you save up over the years. I also just like to see the numbers get bigger and bigger in my bank account.

—SAMMY G., 18

Pivotals aren't simply frugal: They're also out to find the best value. In a recent interview with *Business Insider*, Marcie Merriman, executive director of growth strategy and retail innovation at Ernst & Young, said, "They look beyond just what the price says it is to what you're going to get for it [the price]—are you going to get free delivery? What other services come along with it?"

PIVOTALS BELIEVE IN. . .

Family

Unlike teens of other generations, Pivotals trust the wisdom of their parents and unabashedly share common interests. Teens and their parents frequently enjoy the same music, movies, and TV shows (although Pivotals stream rather than watch cable or satellite). Instead of being embarrassed by parental proximity, many Pivotals actually take pleasure in time spent together. At least, when they have time between social engagements.

"I have my parents on everything." Ellie B., 18, is a Pivotal who falls directly in line with a trend of parental involvement. "I like them knowing what's up in my life. I don't post anything weird or private. I think that speaks more to my relationship with my parents than anything else."

GEN X PARENTING (vs.) BOOMER PARENTING

Protecting through surveillance	Protecting through involvement
What's best for *my* child	What's best for the group of children
Teaching children how to be successful	Giving children what they need to be successful
Realistic—do what you're good at	Aspirations—you can do anything
Only the best win	Everyone wins

Figure 1-6   Gen X parenting versus Boomer parenting.[19]

It's fascinating to compare parenting styles of generations, specifically the attitudes and attributes of their children. The chart in Figure 1-6, adapted from "The First Generation of the Twenty-First Century," by Magid, shows some major differences between Boomers (the parents of Millennials) and Gen X (Pivotals' parents).

The parenting style of Gen X has created a deep appreciation of family in their offspring. Coincidently, according to the 2016 "We Are Gen Z Report" from Sensis, the most prominent Pivotal role models are their parents, specifically moms. Sensis says this is especially the case for Hispanic and African American Pivotals. More than 80 percent of these Pivotals see their parents—in lieu of celebrities and public figures—as the heroes and heroines of their life story.

Diversity and Equality

The first presidential primary election many of us remember was in 2008, when Hillary Clinton, a woman, took on Barack Obama, an African-American man. For us, it has seemed that anything is possible.

—**GRACE MASBACK** , *THE VOICE OF GEN Z:
UNDERSTANDING THE ATTITUDES & ATTRIBUTES
OF AMERICA'S NEXT "GREATEST GENERATION"*

Every generation has a defining cause that serves as the foundation for their behavior. For Boomers, it was antiestablishment. For Millennials, it was the environment. For Pivotals, it is human equality.

According to a national survey of college freshmen, "The American Freshman: National Norms Fall 2015," U.S. students are the most politically and socially engaged they've been since the poll launched 50 years ago. Pivotals readily rally behind racial equality, gender equality, and sexual-orientation equality. The common thread throughout these issues is the relation to the overarching theme of identity. (See Figure 1-7.)

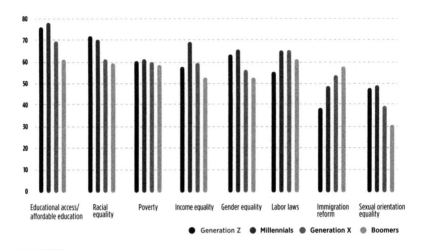

Figure 1-7   Social importance by generation.[20]

While teens are not at a point in their lives where they have had visibility into other socially charged discussions like immigration reform, labor laws, and income equality, most teens today have participated in some sort of discourse about race, gender, and sexual orientation.

As the most ethnically diverse generation in history, Pivotals have grown up in a world where the barriers between races are increasingly blurred. Pivotals embrace the idea of "seeing color" and celebrating their differences rather than pretending that they don't exist or, worse, allowing those differences to cause conflict.

Also, in contrast to their more traditional attitudes, Pivotals are incredibly far-left when it comes to equal rights. A study by FTI Consulting found that 75 percent of voting-age members of the Pivotal generation favor marriage equality and that 83 percent favor equal rights for transgender people.[21] Another study indicates that Pivotals utterly defy the gender binary, with only 48 percent of respondents saying they identified as 100 percent heterosexual, compared with 65 percent of Millennials.[22]

SUCCESS MUST BE EARNED

I believe if something is hard and you have a lot of grit and determination to get it, it will all be worth it. That will be the true satisfaction of working to get there.

—LIAM H., 17

More than half of the teens we surveyed agree that personal success is the most important thing in life. This is nearly 10 percent higher than Millennials. (See Figure 1-8.) A huge reason for this shift in importance of personal success is the influence of social media. When something good happens or if someone experiences a success, sharing the news on social media is expected.

In fact, the Pivotal generation is changing the old saying, "No news is good news." Today, the motto is, "Pics or it didn't happen." By placing such high importance on personal success, Pivotals are ensuring that they do indeed have proof of good news to share.

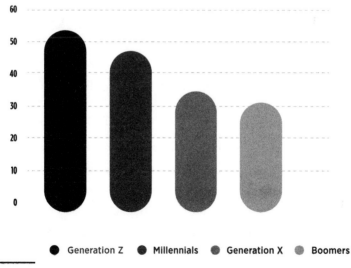

● Generation Z　● Millennials　● Generation X　● Boomers

Figure 1-8　Importance of personal success by generation.[23]

Additionally, this is a group that has ever known only a stagnant economy still responding to the Great Recession. During the height of the economic upheaval, when it came to spending, the Millennial mindset was often, "It's not worth it." There was a sense that spending on material items beyond the necessities was not a worthy way to spend hard earned dollars. As a result, we started to see experiences trump things. Millennials are more experience oriented than any other generation.

Gen Z, however, has shifted this way of thinking from "It's not worth it" to "You have to earn it."

Pivotals view life through a practical lens. They were born into an age where failure is broadcasted almost as much, if not more than success. According to a study conducted by Pew Research Center, there can be as many as 17 negative news reports for every positive one. Pivotals are growing up more aware of failure—making success an even greater aspirational goal. Pivotals are not naive in understanding what it takes to achieve their goals.

According to our research, 69 percent of teens believe becoming successful has little or nothing to do with luck. This isn't surprising, considering that Gen X parents, who are notorious for having a more skeptical and cynical view of the world, raised these teens with an understanding that anything worth achieving takes hard work.

In true form, Pivotals are significantly more likely to say winning individual awards is important. For the Pivotal generation, success is a deeply personal endeavor dependent on individual hard work and achievement.

We see this proven even further when we consider where Pivotals place importance, When asked to rank the topics that were most important in their lives, grades were far and beyond the most important thing, closely tailed only by college admittance.

While this may reflect life stage, it is also an indication of a new mentality shaping our youth today. Pivotals watched Millennials fail while "pursuing their passion." Thus, we are seeing a motivated and

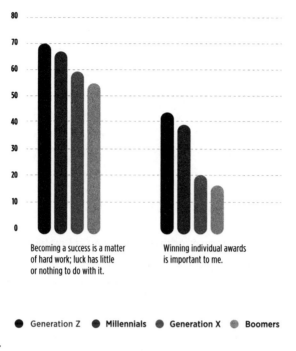

80
70
60
50
40
30
20
10
0

Becoming a success is a matter
of hard work; luck has little
or nothing to do with it.

Winning individual awards
is important to me.

● Generation Z ● Millennials ● Generation X ● Boomers

Figure 1-9 Achievement beliefs by generation.[24]

grounded generation come of age—one that echoes a traditional sentiment of personal achievement. (See Figure 1-9.)

HARNESS THEIR POWER

In summary, like the Millennial generation before them, the Pivotal generation is once again forcing brands to rethink what it means to connect with consumers in a modern era. Pivotals are a proud crew; they value their intelligence, diversity, common sense, and family. They believe in hard work and understand that technology is yet another tool to make their work more efficient.

As we saw in Kate Jackson's daily life, Pivotals have a lot on their plate. They're willing to do whatever it takes to succeed, and they are not above asking for help. Pivotals will look to those they trust for guidance, input, and support. This openness is the perfect opportunity for brands to step in and create real, lasting value.

With this in mind, let's explore how you can best prepare your organization to succeed. We admit, there is no secret formula or insider tip that best attracts Pivotals, but there are key insights that will help you befriend the most influential and sophisticated consumer group yet.

KEY TAKEAWAYS

- **The most fitting term for this generation is Pivotals.** They are pivoting away from common Millennial behaviors and attitudes and veering toward a socially conscious and diverse era.

- **Pivotals are old souls in young bodies.** Earnest, hardworking, and driven by conservative views of success regarding money, education, and career advancement, Gen Zers resemble a much older generation.

- **To Pivotals, technology should be invisible.** It's all about speed and a seamless user experience. If Pivotals notice the technology, you're doing something wrong.

- **For Pivotals, equality is non-negotiable.** Pivotals celebrate their differences. They will hold their favorite brands to the same standards they set for themselves regarding equality and acceptance.

- **Pivotals can smell marketing from a mile away.** Forget "always be closing" and think "always be collaborating"—the new ABCs of marketing require collaboration with a savvy consumer who expects it.

MOBILE AND SOCIAL FROM BIRTH

Millennials adapted to technology as they got older, starting with laptops, then iPods and iPads, then the iPhone, etc. But Gen Z is the first truly digital generation—the first generation who could FaceTime their friends, text their mom and order a pizza, all at the same time.

—CONNOR BLAKLEY

For older generations, it seems Pivotals came out of the womb with the ability to pinch, swipe, and zoom. While an obvious exaggeration, isn't it a tad suspect we don't remember teaching any of these behaviors?

Yet somehow Pivotals learned to swipe before they could even speak. Attempting to swipe the unswipable—like TV screens or the pages of a magazine—they assumed the image in front of them was "broken."

Perhaps it's because instead of settling their developing minds in front of a TV to watch *Sesame Street*, parents handed toddler Pivotals a smartphone or tablet for entertainment in the car, at a restaurant, or when mom and dad needed a break. Entertainment didn't happen just in the living room: It was in the palm of their hands at all times.

So it should come as no surprise that Pivotals are, without a doubt, mobile-first. They have never known a world without smartphones, tablets, and immediate access to the Internet. A 2017 IBM Institute for Business Value study in collaboration with the National Retail Federation found that 75 percent of young consumers surveyed selected their mobile phone as their device of choice, largely because of their desire for always-on connection to the Internet and social media. (See Figure 2-1.)

For many Pivotals, their first "selfies" were sonogram photos. They made their first digital footprint before they took their first step. We're not joking. More than 90 percent of Pivotals have staked out their

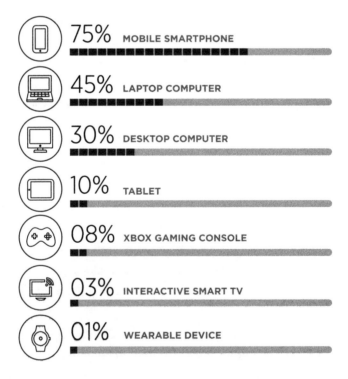

Figure 2-1   Most frequently used devices.[1]

digital territory,[2] and most can thank their parents for starting them out young.

While most parents post photos of their children on their own accounts, another significant percentage of parents go so far as to create Instagram accounts in their child's name and even post *as* the child. This concept has created a source of controversy for parents caught between oversharing and wanting to protect their child.

Since then, social media has been Pivotals' constant companion, documenting their daily lives—everything from family to school to dating—all while influencing how they view the world. Pivotals simultaneously trust the familiar digital world, while also craving distance from constant exposure. This contradiction developed a generation of confidence and insecurity, connectedness and privacy.

Because they've never known a world without it, technology and social media is also interchangeable and invisible. Social media is neither a technological breakthrough nor "media." It's simply "social"— the most convenient way to live a social life. It's how they connect with friends and family, relate to the world, and have fun.

However, it won't be enough to simply transfer traditional advertising approaches, commercials, or messages into tomorrow's social media campaigns. Reaching Pivotals in this space will require creativity, flexibility, and perseverance as they continue to create and shape social media to meet their needs and fit seamlessly into their busy lives.

THEIR SOCIAL LIFE STORY

Human civilization has always been averse to technological advances. Even Socrates opposed the development of writing, convinced that knowledge can be gained only through dialogue. The classical philosopher contended that writing something down causes one's memory of the event to become distorted and one-dimensional. Regardless, writing became a staple of our civilization, and society progressed.

The Internet, too, spawned controversy regarding its potential to dumb us down. After the Web became ingrained in everyday life, the rise of social media brought along similar concerns about its negative impact on humanity. But despite the bells and whistles, social media is merely a tool that enables natural social behavior, albeit on a massive scale.

That said, there are obvious downsides. Social media directly impacts how individuals view themselves. With some 13-year-olds checking their social accounts as many as 100 times per day, according to the #Being13 study conducted exclusively by CNN, researchers have warned of potential addiction issues. Other studies say it causes self-esteem issues and even depression (more on this in Chapter 5).

Parents, educators, and mental health professionals alike continue to question whether social media is a positive or negative influence on Pivotals, especially since so many are still teenagers developing their personal identities. There are adamant arguments on both sides of this debate.

Journalist Nancy Jo Sales, author of *American Girls: Social Media and the Secret Lives of Teenagers*, says social media allows some teens to feel more empowered and connected, whereas others fall victim to cyberbullying. With its prevalence as a tool for daily peer interactions, social media impacts young users in both positive and negative ways.

In a 2016 blog post, marketing expert and entrepreneur Gary Vaynerchuk said, "Technology has not changed us, it just makes it easy to engage in behaviors that we would rather be doing anyway."

To those concerned about Pivotals' ability to socialize and their perceived disconnectness from the real world, Vaynerchuk would argue, "Children who have 'no friends' in school now have the opportunity to make online friends through social platforms." On the Internet, finding like-minded individuals and communities to connect with is no more than a click away.[3]

Vaynerchuk also has a convincing argument about the evolution of technology. "Every new medium brings along a healthy fear that the newest invention will ruin society. But, the truth is that people will always be looking for new ways to be entertained, consume media, and engage with each other."[4]

Calm, Cool, and Connected

With tools like FaceTime, Snapchat, Skype, and Google Hangouts, Pivotals may be the *most* connected generation in history. They don't need to be in the same location to communicate "in full sight, sound, and motion."[5] Imagine if we (adults over 30) had the same tools at our disposal as teens. Our social lives would have been off the hook!

While Pivotals use their mobile devices for many tasks, 73 percent cited texting and chatting as their primary mobile phone activity, per the 2017 IBM study in collaboration with the National Retail Federation.[6] This points to their desire and basic human need to connect. The same study also shows their overall use of social media centers around a tight circle of friends and family, where they express themselves by posting comments on friends' posts and sharing photos and videos, opinions, and links to songs and playlists.

In their book, *The Gen Z Effect*, Koulopoulos and Keldsen warn us that "swimming against the Gen Z tide of hyperconnectivity is like swimming against a tsunami." We must not view "hyperconnectivity as [a] distraction" but instead, see it as Gen Z does: as a way to engage and build relationships.

Experiences

Driven by a need for social recognition, Pivotals seek out opportunities to be seen doing fun and exciting activities, like attending concerts and sporting events, going out to eat, traveling, or just hanging out in trendy places with their friends.

A 2016 study by Retail Perceptions reports 62 percent of Pivotals prefer to spend their money on an experience rather than on something material. Back to the need for human interaction—nearly half (47 percent) say they spend money each week on experiences with friends, making it one of the leading spending categories for teens.[7]

"Social media is only fueled by how good your actual social life is, and Pivotals have a very profound knowledge of this," explains Joe Cox, engagement director at Barkley. "They're collectors of experiences

Figure 2-2 Illustration inspired by Chompoo Baritone's Instagram Effect photo series.

and use it to further their social currency with friends and people in social circles."

Social media drives this pressure to present the coolest version of themselves, otherwise known as the "Instagram effect."

This effect isn't a mysterious phenomenon. Teens will openly admit to taking countless photos in an attempt to get the best shot. Chompoo Baritone, a Bangkok-based photographer fascinated with the Instagram effect, created a series to illustrate it that swept through the digital sphere. (See Figure 2-2.)

Her photos show the reality of what's just outside the perfectly cropped frame. Pivotals related to the collection of photos and unabashedly shared it among their networks. While funny and a bit ridiculous, Baritone's work is a rather serious reflection of the value placed on an interesting and photo-worthy social life. Her work and the acceptance by the very group it criticizes point to a generation of ambitious yet authentic spirits.

Education

Pivotals have developed a reputation not only for their adept learning abilities, but also for seeking out and enjoying educational opportunities. Further enabling this insatiable desire for education—or perhaps the underlying cause of it—are technology and mobile access. With a wealth of instant information at their fingertips, wasn't it inevitable?

Angie recalls a story of checking in on her then 17-year-old son, who was supposed to be studying. Expecting to find him sitting at his desk with open books and paper scattered about, instead she found him sprawled out on his bed, with his laptop open, TV on, and his smartphone in hand. She reacted as most parents might, with a few harsh words of warning that he needed to stop messing around and start studying. He turned to her and said, "Mom, I *am* studying."

And he was. His study guide was pulled up on his laptop, he was researching something on his phone, and the TV served as ambient noise. In that moment, Angie realized the "old school" learning environment—her version of studying—had changed dramatically.

Educators are jumping on board, too (although some students complain they're not doing so fast enough). Pivotals are practicing mathematics and fine-tuning their writing skills online, and per a Sparks & Honey study, 52 percent use YouTube to supplement their online courses.[8] Teachers and students leverage dedicated software, as well as mobile apps, making educational apps the third largest category in the iTunes app store.[9]

Quizlet, a popular educational app and website, offers free flashcards and study games to learn course material. Since their core demographic is students, one-third of Quizlet users are 18 or younger.[10] Duolingo, another favorite that lives perennially in the top five education apps on iTunes, provides language-learning games to improve reading, writing, and speaking skills in one of 23 languages.

What can brands take from this? Feed Pivotals' desire for constant education and self-improvement. Provide a valuable utility somehow, whether it involves developing a skill or introducing them to contemporary ideas and trends. This is a generation that loves to learn, so find a way to make it easy for them.

Change the World

One of the characteristics we love most about Pivotals is their genuine desire to make a difference—to change the world. Community consciousness is a defining characteristic of this generation. They've even been called "Philanthro*teens*." They're not simply dreaming about making a difference "someday in the future." They're already doing it, and they're using social media to help.

More than one million people, many of them Pivotals, "checked into" the Standing Rock Indian Reservation page on Facebook to raise awareness for the tribe and protesters fighting against the implementation of the Dakota Access Pipeline.

Remember the ALS Ice Bucket Challenge? That, too, was a viral social media phenomenon. Users, including Pivotals, participated by dumping a bucket full of ice-cold water over their heads and sharing the shrieking footage on Facebook. Participants, after drying off, donated to ALS research and challenged their friends to do the same within 24 hours. In total, the ALS Ice Bucket Challenge raised $220 million worldwide for advancements in research.[11]

Grace Masback thinks Pivotals' strong sense of community consciousness is one of the silver linings of living through the Great Recession:

> We've seen what economic hardship can do to families, communities and the world around us. Because we want to leave the world better than we found it, community service is now the expected norm, not just something we're obligated to do through school, church, family, etc. We care about giving back and want to do it right here, right now.

In her book, Masback shares the story of her friend Nadya Okamoto, an 18-year-old from Portland, Oregon, and the founder and executive director of Camions of Care (now called PERIOD. The Menstrual Movement). During her freshman year of college, Nadya started PERIOD, a youth-run, global nonprofit that strives to manage and celebrate menstrual hygiene through advocacy, youth leadership, and service—primarily through the global distribution of feminine hygiene products. Nadya uses Facebook, Twitter, and Instagram to raise awareness about the organization and spread the word about how to get involved, including starting chapters in local communities around the country.

There are thousands more like Nadya. While not every Pivotal will take it as far as she and her ambitious cohorts, as a generation, they are wired to give back. The 2015 Cassandra report on U.S./U.K. teens shows 49 percent of teens volunteer at least once a month and 20 percent even want to start their own charity someday.[12] While they're a frugal bunch, they'll put their money where their mouths (and hearts) are. The same Cassandra report shows 26 percent have raised money for a cause and 32 percent have donated their own money. What's more, 39 percent see giving time and money to charity as a "measure of success."

Seventeen-year-old Lulu Cerone even wrote a book about throwing "parties with a purpose." In *PhilanthroParties! A Party-Planning Guide for Kids Who Want to Give Back*, Cerone encourages teens to put the "social" back in social activism and make an impact on their communities in a fun, DIY way.

Recognizing Pivotals' desire to get involved and give back, organizations like DoSomething.org are designed to give young people an easy, virtually turnkey way to change the world. Users can visit the website and select from hundreds of current campaigns and causes, both online and offline. By documenting and proving their involvement (e.g., by sharing a pic or completing an assignment), they can earn points toward scholarships and swag—the tangible measure of success that Pivotals desire.

Brands vying to win with Pivotals can take a cue from DoSomething.org or Boxed Water. These companies strive to make the world a better place and are diligent in putting their corporate needs second.

Boxed Water gained popularity with Pivotals by aligning its product and brand with a deeply held cause. For instance, the Boxed Water slogan, "Boxed Water is Better," appears on every single product.

Why? Because you aren't only buying water—you're supporting sustainability and bettering our earth through the one million trees Boxed Water pledges to plant by 2020.[13]

Gaming

The most obvious form of fun connected to mobile and social media is online gaming, which is huge with Pivotals. So huge, in fact, that upward of 66 percent proudly claim gaming as their main hobby.[14] And despite popular stereotypes, gaming is no longer confined to the basement.

Case in point: Pokémon Go in the summer of 2016 prompted teens—even entire families—to go on walks, phones in hand, in search of Pokémon characters superimposed into their surroundings. Thanks to augmented reality, Pokémon Go created the first real-world-meets-digital, scavenger-hunt style of game.

Only one day after it launched—with minimal traditional marketing support—Pokémon Go was the top game on both Apple's App Store and Google Play. Word of mouth spread quickly on messaging apps and Snapchat rather than via Twitter and Facebook, proving Pivotals were the driving force behind this cultural phenomenon.

Of course, parents are notorious for assuming that playing computer games is a waste of time. But for teens, digital entertainment has become a catalyst for creating and maintaining friendships. In fact, more than 50 percent of teens strike up new friendships online, per a 2015 Pew study.[15]

Giggles

Fun is one thing, *funny* another. Spend five minutes with Pivotals and ask them to show you some funny videos, memes, or GIFs. While you'll get a chuckle from the more predictable cat videos, you'll most likely see something so quirky and oddball, you'll end up scratching your head instead of laughing.

In a 2015 article for *Fast Company*, Scott Fogel, a senior strategist at Firstborn Multimedia Corporation, a design and technology company, says a lot of what Pivotals love has a "weird, unhinged sensibility to it." They love self-deprecating Snapchats and memes, or videos that make them appear to be offbeat or quirky.

Fogel points out this is not a Millennial behavior. "It's rare for a Millennial to post anything on social that makes them look strange. But for a generation that's spent their entire lives online—mostly in the unfiltered lens of Skype, webcams, live streams and vlogs—an intimate exhibitionism has emerged in a way that older generations simply don't have."[16]

Brands that infuse humor and self-deprecation into their personalities will appeal more to Pivotals, but be careful. Don't try to pander to this generation by using too many popular acronyms or teen slang: They will instantly peg you as trying too hard. Amanda Gutterman, VP of growth at digital media company Dose Studios, shared a great analogy in a recent Contently article: "You don't want to come onto a platform like Snapchat and be perceived as someone's weird uncle trying to be cool."[17]

Entertainment and Fun

Last but certainly not least, social media provides an outlet for fun and entertainment. Teens have always been hardwired for celebration and entertainment. Most adults would never want to repeat their teenage years (puberty, peer pressure, homework, tests—ugh!), but aside from those cringe-worthy memories, having fun was always a top priority.

Don't Bet the Farm on Social

While Pivotals have the world in the palm of their hands, it would be a mistake to assume all of them revere social media. Grace Masback personally isn't a fan of social media, and many of her friends feel the same.

In her book, Masback breaks Pivotals down into three categories, the first of whom are those "obsessed with their social life." Socializing is their hobby. You'll likely find these people "glued to their phones, obsessing over Snapchat 'streaks,' and deleting old Instagram photos." The second group cares but isn't "overly concerned" about their social media presence. These Pivotals occasionally share pieces of their lives online or use social media to keep in touch with friends. Finally, the third group are "those who have social media but rarely use it." They use social media only selectively. Kate Jackson (see the Introduction) falls into this category.

Masback also wants brands to recognize a defining characteristic of her generation: They are busy! "We don't have time to spend our whole life on social media. We need to balance school, sports, extracurricular activities, community service, and the businesses we've started."

As FutureCast and Barkley's "Getting to Know Gen Z" report contends, Pivotals know how to keep their priorities straight. They take school seriously, rating grades as their highest priority, followed by getting into a good college. Social media ranks far lower on the list. (See Figure 2-3.)

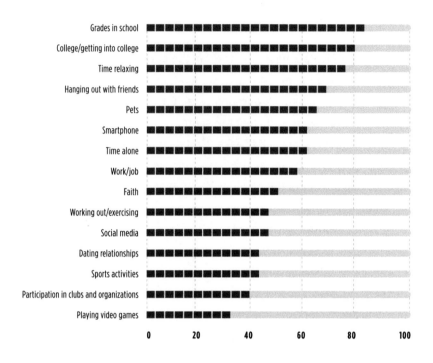

Figure 2-3 Pivotal importance of daily activities.[18]

SOCIAL IRL (IN REAL LIFE)

I definitely prefer seeing my friends in person rather than over social media because I feel closer to them when I really see them. I love to laugh with them and be able to see a genuine reaction rather than an "LOL" over text. How am I supposed to know if they are really laughing or if they just don't know what else to say?

—**GRETA J., 15**

Contrary to popular belief, Pivotals don't always have their noses glued to their phones. The 2017 "Uniquely Generation Z" report showed that socializing is important to Pivotals—both online and off. They also value spending time with family and friends. (See Figure 2-4.)

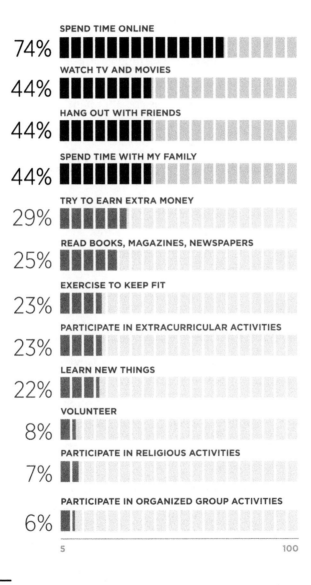

Figure 2-4 Time spent outside of school or work.[19]

According to a 2016 article in *Scientific American* by Nicolas Karda-ras, "Social connection is not only the most essential part of being human; it is also a key ingredient in happiness and health." He con-tends that we are the most connected society ever, due to social media: "Each second people in the U.S. send more than 7,500 tweets, 1,394 Instagram photographs, and two million e-mails; they also view more than 119,000 YouTube videos."[20] Inasmuch as this essential social con-nection can be achieved digitally, it should come as no surprise how strongly social media affects Pivotals' development!

SOCIAL MEDIA EXPECTATIONS

Pivotals expect the ability to fulfill their needs on their own time. That's why on-demand companies that allow consumers to request services at a moment's notice are so popular with this generation.

On-Demand

Hungry? Get food delivered to your door in minutes through Deliv-eroo or Postmates. Mom and Dad too busy to give you a lift some-where? No worries—Uber or Lyft has your back. Need to veg out for a bit? Netflix or Hulu enables your inner couch potato, on your schedule. Plus, while you're at it, how about a date-on-demand through Tinder? OK, maybe that's pushing it, especially for teenag-ers, but you get the point.

Unfortunately, with nearly everything available at the touch of a button, Pivotals aren't the most patient people. Surveys show they are emerging as the heaviest users of on-demand services around the world.[21] Brands beware—they're likely to be the most demanding con-sumers you've ever seen. The 2017 IBM study showed 60 percent of those surveyed will not use an app or website that is too slow to load.

Pivotals expect instant gratification, and marketers have no choice but to adapt to this expectation.

Speed isn't the only factor playing into Pivotals' expectations. Gen Zers' desire for brand transparency extends to their social media preferences as well.

Authenticity

It's time to get real. Pivotals are moving toward platforms that encourage and celebrate authenticity, and they expect brands to do the same.

In a 2016 *Fortune* article, Gregg Witt, executive vice president of youth marketing at Motivate Youth, tells Connor Blakley "The first and most prominent mistake I see brands make via their social media strategies is that they create an ingenious character to represent their image. Gen Z wants real. Gen Z wants transparency. And Gen Z wants originality."[22]

Witt says brands can take cues from Levi's. Levi's is strategic about whom it selects as brand ambassadors. Instead of looking for the most popular influencers or the ones with the highest followers, Levi's instead tries to find individuals who fit its brand DNA. "It takes a clever blend of realness and relatability for brands targeting teens to be successful," Witt said.[23] We'll talk more about that in Chapter 4.

Privacy and Anonymity

Pivotals learned from an early age, both from their parents and in school, the importance of online privacy and security. It's been pounded into them. As a result, they are acutely aware of what is and isn't okay to share online.

One of the first things they do when turning on their phones or logging into a social app is to enable their privacy settings. Plus, they are good at policing themselves online. They know embarrassing photos or rants can live online forever, potentially hurting their chances with their dream colleges and employers down the road.

A few years ago, rumor had it that Pivotals would be making a mass exodus from social media. Celebrities like Lena Dunham and Jaden Smith deleted their social media accounts because of the emotional turmoil of online haters. But instead of leaving, Pivotals simply transitioned to more private, anonymous, and temporary options, like Snapchat and Whisper. They're also flocking toward the "dark social"—messenger. That's why the Facebooks and Instagrams of the world are placing big bets on messaging apps.

Privacy is one of the main reasons Snapchat is so popular among Pivotals. First, it allows users to share messages and images, then deletes them within seconds. Also, it more closely resembles face-to-face interaction, which remains important to Pivotals. You have a "conversation" and then it's gone.[24]

Whisper allows users to send messages anonymously and receive anonymous replies. Posts, known as "whispers," contain text overlaid on images. Users don't have to publicly identify themselves, which gives them more freedom to express their thoughts and opinions on topics they might not otherwise feel comfortable talking about with people they know.

Both Snapchat and Whisper offer advertising opportunities, but connecting with Pivotals through incognito apps is tricky and will continue to be a learning process for marketers. The key will be finding a way to appeal to users, who want to feel like people—not marketing targets—in a way that doesn't come off as an intrusion or "selling."

FOMO and FOLO

As already mentioned, some 13-year-olds check their social media accounts 100 times a day and spend about nine hours a day using media for their enjoyment. To put this into perspective, that is more time than most teens spend sleeping or with their parents/teachers, and it does not account for the media used at school or while doing their homework.

"I think they're addicted to the peer connection and affirmation they're able to get via social media," said child clinical psychologist Marion Underwood, coauthor of the #Being13 study in an interview with CNN. "To know what each other are doing, where they stand, to know how many people like what they posted, to know how many people followed them today and unfollowed them . . . that, I think, is highly addictive."

The study proceeded to explore why teens felt the need to regulate their social media and what it found is highly indicative of a generation riddled with FOMO (fear of missing out) and FOLO (fear of living offline). More than half of teens in the study wanted to see if they were receiving likes and comments, and over a third wanted to see if their friends were getting together without them. Twenty-one percent wanted to confirm that nobody was saying hurtful things about them.[25]

While this may be a reflection of life stage, we tend to believe this is more revealing of a generation that has been guided by social media and digital technology their whole lives. As a result, they routinely fret about how their digital lives and identities impact their relationships with others in real life.

New Rules for Social

Every day, it seems another company launches a Snapchat account to reach a younger audience. Some have even started posting "behind the scenes" Snapchat stories to promote their products, a format so overused, it feels unoriginal and uninspiring.

—CONNOR BLAKLEY, "HOW TO BUILD A MARKETING CAM-
PAIGN THAT APPEALS TO GENERATION Z"[26]

As mentioned in the previous section, these worries about how Pivotals' digital identities impact their real lives have led to the formation of etiquette that governs individual social media platforms. Using social media is not, as it turns out, a free-for-all. In focus groups conducted by FutureCast, we worked with teens to learn why they use various social media accounts (focusing on the big four: Facebook, Twitter, Instagram, and Snapchat) and what they use them for. We learned that Pivotals adhere to a detailed system of rules and guidelines for each platform.

Facebook

Contrary to popular belief, Facebook is not dead among Pivotals. Yes, their use of Facebook is declining, but it is still the most used social media platform, with 77 percent of teens saying they use Facebook on a regular basis. (Millennials are still the most likely to use Facebook on a regular basis at 87 percent.)

But notice that we say "used," not "engaged." There's a difference. With the primary demographic of Facebook aging (thanks, Mom and Dad . . . oh, and Grandma), teens today are less likely to be actively engaged with the platform's shared content. Originally, Facebook was *the* engagement tool. Now teens are more likely to use Facebook as a passive tool—a jumping-off point. They scroll rather than post. This is turning Facebook into more of an information hub than a networking platform.

But that doesn't mean brands should ignore Facebook as a way to interact with Pivotals. If done correctly and with a bit of creativity, it still has the potential to capture their attention.

For example, Playland at the PNE, a Canadian amusement park, gave eight teenagers free passes under the condition that Facebook fans could control the experience of those in the "hot seat." Fans at home dictated the rides ridden, games played, and even food eaten by the contestants, who wore GoPro cameras to broadcast their experiences. The video content engaged more than 28,000 teenagers on Facebook in real time.

Twitter

Twitter is the "be on" platform. Often used for real-time marketing, Twitter is where teens go to get information now. The life expectancy of a tweet that has been retweeted is no more than 18 minutes (tweets that have not been retweeted have a decreased life expectancy of only a few minutes). Per our research, Pivotals lead Twitter usage at 45 percent compared to 34 percent for Millennials and Gen X and just 13 percent for Boomers.

When 16-year-old Carter Wilkerson tweeted Wendy's asking how many retweets would get him free chicken nuggets for a year, the fast-food chain responded, "18 million." Wilkerson accepted the challenge and began soliciting retweets with the hashtag #NuggsforCarter. (See Figure 2-5.) Big-name celebrities and corporations such as Ellen DeGeneres, Amazon, and Microsoft promoted the tweet, encouraging their followers to support the movement. Wilkerson used the campaign buzz to start a fundraiser for the Dave Thomas Foundation for Adoption and Pinocchio's Moms on the Run.

After the tweet became the most retweeted of all time, Wendy's gave in to Wilkerson's demand and granted him a year of free chicken nuggets and donated $100,000 to Wilkerson's fundraiser. Wendy's, by simply engaging with a customer on social media, has received widespread positive media coverage. As the fast-food brand has been widely recognized for their snarky Twitter usage over the years, the interactions with Wilkerson felt completely on-brand.

■   ■   ■

Figure 2-5 Rendering of Carter Wilkerson's chicken nugget challenge to Wendy's.

Instagram

Per our research, Pivotals lead Instagram usage at 63 percent, compared to 47 percent of Millennials—a dramatic difference. Instagram is where teens go to be inspired. They spend time editing their images and creating the most aspirational versions of themselves. Teens are very careful about how they use their Instagram accounts.

When it comes to posting, they want to be sure they are not clogging their friends' feeds with low-quality images (that's what Snapchat is for). They also regularly delete their Instagram photos so their profiles rarely have more than a handful at any given time; this is intended to optimize the number of likes per photo.

Retailer Aeropostale manages to get more than 100,000 comments and likes per post by maintaining a balance of candid and aspirational Instagram photos. The brand avoids too many product-heavy photos and instead mixes in ice cream cones, flower fields, and friends on the beach to tell a story with an emotional connection.

Snapchat

Given their desire for personal connectivity—wanting to actually see their friends as they talk online—Snapchat has become the go-to app for Pivotals.[27] Snapchat allows manually selected recipients a peek into a user's reality, rather than sharing a picture-perfect moment. Again, Pivotals lead Snapchat usage at 61 percent compared to 34 percent of Millennials and few Gen Xers, and Snapchat is very quickly replacing texting.

According to our teens, it is the perfect way to let people know what they're doing in the moment. Being mobile-first, Gen Z prefers Snapchat and Instagram because these apps were also built mobile-first, meaning the user experience is cleaner, is more useful, and requires less jumping around from app to app.

CASE STUDY

WHO: Taco Bell

WHAT: On Cinco de Mayo 2016, the fast food brand launched a Snapchat filter that transformed users' heads into giant tacos. (See Figure 2-6.)

HOW: The filter—complete with the signature Taco Bell bong noise and logo in the corner—entertained users for an average of 24 seconds before they sent the snap. Taco Bell reportedly spent around $750,000 for the day-long campaign.

IMPACT: In unique plays, the filter generated 12.5 years of play in a single day! Snapchat advertising allows users to interact with the content and share it with friends, making them more likely to remember it. At 224 million views, Taco Bell broke the existing record for a Snapchat campaign.[28]

Figure 2-6   Illustration of Taco Bell's Cinco de Mayo Snapchat filter.

SUMMING UP SOCIAL

A 2015 MediaPost article likens social media to the mall, encouraging brands to have a storefront there if they want to connect with Pivotals.[29] Unfortunately, figuring out the what, where, when, and how of building that storefront is a moving target, which requires savvy marketing teams that understand Pivotals' latest rules of social media and how to find the appropriate balance of authenticity, frequency, humor, and brand messaging.

In an interview with *Campaign*, Lucie Greene, worldwide director of JWT Intelligence, suggested embracing Gen Z's hyperawareness of marketing. "They've been marketed to their whole life, not just through linear advertising but through guerrilla marketing, bloggers, viral sensations, and social media phenomenon, which over the years have all become co-opted by brands." Due to this lifelong exposure, Gen Z has an uncanny ability to pick out brands "producing even a hint of self-interest" and disregard them.[30]

It will be critical for marketing teams to fully understand both the purpose and pitfalls of each social channel, then make strategic content choices based on what Pivotals expect to see in each one. Again, a one-size-fits-all approach won't work. Unless your brand fits seamlessly into their lives, provides a utility, or solves a problem, blatant advertising of any kind turns Pivotals off completely.

"Social media of the future will allow users to even be more fluid and to get to the most valuable content the quickest, without having to jump around or navigate so manually," predicts Joe Cox.

═══ **KEY TAKEAWAYS** ═══

■ **Pivotals are mobile-first.** They have never known a world without smartphones, tablets, and immediate access to the Internet.

■ **Pivotals simultaneously trust the familiar digital world, while also craving distance from constant exposure.** This contradiction developed a generation of confidence and insecurity, connectedness, and privacy.

■ **Pivotals may be the most connected generation in history.** With tools like FaceTime, Snapchat, Skype, and Google Hangouts, they don't need to be in the same location to communicate in full sight, sound, and motion.

■ **Pivotals use social media to amplify their IRL social lives, educate themselves, make the world a better place, and to have fun and be entertained.** And they expect on-demand, authentic, and private/anonymous experiences.

■ **Pivotals adhere to a detailed system of rules and guidelines for each platform.** Using social media is not a free-for-all.

NEW COMMUNICATION RULES

Cave paintings. Egyptian hieroglyphics. Geoglyphs in Peru.

Visual communication isn't just in our history; it's hardwired into our brains. We've evolved, yes. We moved from stone walls to touch screens, but the method remains the same. We connect, relate, and respond best to visual communication. We have to see it to believe it.

Whereas Millennials perfected the art of the written word (aka texting), Pivotals communicate with symbols, videos, GIFs, and emojis. Smartphones, video games, and streaming video have taken this generation back to their ancestral roots. For marketers, this means creating content centered around quick entertainment without compromising quality.

■　■　■

GO MOBILE OR GO HOME

I got my first cell phone when I was in the fifth grade. I was very excited. I was like, "Oh my god, this is the most important thing that's ever happened to me." Kids my age—it's an enormous part of our lives.

—DAVID F., 14

Pivotals aren't mobile-*first*, they're mobile-*only*. To them, a phone isn't just a phone. In fact, it can hardly be considered a "phone" at all, as they rarely make actual voice calls. Instead, it's a personal portal between their offline and online worlds. Getting their first phone is right up there with their first kiss, getting their driver's license, and graduation. It's a rite of passage for today's youth.

As a result, good luck finding a teenager without a smartphone. They've become the latest place setting at the dinner table. Teens keep them within arm's reach while showering. They even sleep with them. This, of course, gives parents and educators a migraine. Are we raising a "heads-down" generation of mobile-addicted robots?

But this phenomenon isn't limited to teens. Most of us can admit to keeping our phones on our nightstands. You may even be reading this book from your mobile device. But it hasn't always been this way.

Members of the Gen X and Boomer generations didn't have a cell phone until well into their twenties or later. They learned to depend on cell phones over time. While exposed to the mobility of cell phones much earlier (middle school and high school were typical for most), Millennials didn't even have the same early exposure as Gen Z. Pivotals were *born* into a mobile world. Years before they got their own personal phones (around the age of 12), they were playing games or watching videos on Mom's or Dad's device. The screen was just as consoling as a pacifier.

With nearly constant visual stimulation since birth, Pivotals learn with their eyes first. What marketers used to call the "third screen," the mobile phone, is Pivotals' first—and in many cases *only*—screen. They use their phones instead of laptops, home computers, and TVs to get their news, information, and entertainment. Everything they need is already in the palm of their hand.

The Big Impact of Small and Fast

With this unprecedented visual access to the outside world, Pivotals challenge marketers, educators, and parents to join them on their smaller screens. This young generation moves fast and thinks even faster.

So what type of content works best for catching these cyber cheetahs? Certainly not lines and lines of text.

What works best is, unsurprisingly, *speed.* Hence the importance of visual assets. Images. Short, punchy text. Quick and compelling videos. Customized, personal messages. In fact, Pivotals are conditioned to handle mass amounts of visual stimuli. Studies even suggest that their brains have evolved to process more information at faster speeds.[1] There's no sense in fighting it. Even educators are getting on board and allowing mobile phones in school.

Many teachers are now structuring their lessons in what's called the "flipped classroom." Teachers record their lectures and make them available to students online. Actual class time serves as a space for collaboration and discussion. When a teacher says, "look it up," phones are the new dictionary, encyclopedia, and thesaurus all in one.

Due to their comfort level with mobile, Pivotals also aren't shy about making purchases from their phones. While older generations are just now comfortable making online purchases across industries, from apparel to tech to auto (really—it's not abnormal to see a new set of tires shipped to the office by a co-worker short on time), many are still reluctant to do so from their phones. On the other hand, 53 percent of teens between 13 and 17 usually make online purchases from their smartphones, according to a study from Google.[2] Even when they're in a retail store (yes, they still shop in brick-and-mortar stores, as we'll discuss in Chapter 6), they are using their phones to compare prices and perform additional research.

What does this mean for marketers? First, if you haven't already embraced a mobile-friendly communications strategy, you're late to the game. With Pivotals, it really is a matter of "go mobile or go home."

If Pivotals have to whip out their laptop to interact with your brand online, you're going to lose them. Can you say or show something in 10 seconds instead of 30? Will it capture their attention in that elusive eight-second filter? You have to consider the type of content you're producing on behalf of your brand. What's going to play best on mobile?

Google search results now favor websites that are mobile optimized as opposed to simply mobile friendly. Mobile-*friendly* designs resize content to fit any device's screen dimensions, which is increasingly relevant as phones continue to grow in screen size. However, mobile *optimized* means the site was designed to target mobile users, incorporating features such as a single-column layout, minimalist design, and simple navigation. (See Figure 3-1.)

Websites originally designed for the mobile user are called "mobile-first," with desktop as a secondary concern. StatCounter, a global data aggregator, estimates mobile usage first surpassed desktop in 2016.[3] We've moved past mere accommodation; brands must optimize for the smaller screen from the ground up if they expect to appeal to younger consumers.

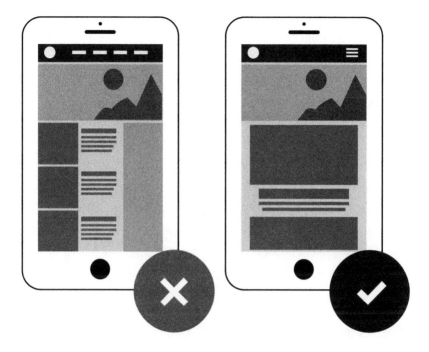

Figure 3-1 Rendering of mobile-first design.

CASE STUDY

Who: Mountain Dew

What: The brand launched a mobile-first global campaign featuring videos of athletes in action. Pro skateboarder Sean Malto starred in the first video spot, soaring over a car in slow motion. The campaign's tagline, "There's No Feeling Like Doing," focuses on the exhilarating sensation of "doing" rather than on the action itself.

How: The campaign, designed for mobile, used Twitter, Snapchat, Facebook Live, Facebook Video, and Instagram Stories to create a more visually focused experience and to encourage consumers to share their own exciting activities. Not only did the brand change its strategy, but it updated its visual identity and slogan as well.

Impact: Having mobile at the forefront of this campaign is what made Mountain Dew's strategy so innovative. The brand pursued this mobile-first marketing direction to capture the attention of younger consumers who live as a mobile-first generation.

"It's no longer about figuring out how creative can be optimized for mobile at the end of production, but now how it can be designed to thrive in mobile from the outset," said Greg Lyons, SVP of marketing, Mountain Dew, North America.[4]

Bite-Sized = Right-Sized

We tell our advertising partners that if they don't communicate in five words and a big picture, they will not reach this generation.

—DAN SCHAWBEL, IN AN INTERVIEW WITH *THE NEW YORK TIMES* [5]

What do we mean when we say "bite-sized" or "snackable" content? Snackable content, according to Meg Cannistra of Ceros, is comprised of three key ingredients: It's eye-catching, it's short, and it's easy to follow.[6]

With so many media channels, Pivotals are bombarded with marketing messages every minute of the day. No human, let alone a teen, has the time or the patience to process everything, so to cut through the clutter, information needs to be direct, quick, and simple.

Remember the KISS principle? Keep it simple, stupid. But don't confuse simple with easy. It takes a lot of work to boil things down to their simplest elements. It's a lot easier to explain something in 500 characters than 140 or in 30 seconds versus 10. (See Figure 3-2.) Or in 100 words instead of 10. Or, as Dan Schawbel contends, five words!

Preference for mobile is one thing, but attention span is an entirely different monster. Pivotals are distracted and often lack the time or tolerance to absorb long-form information.

Mobile not only makes it easy to consume small bites of content but also gives Pivotals the freedom to consume on *their* time. Pivotals have never known a world without instant consumption of snackable content, day or night.

Figure 3-2 Snackable content by social media platform. At time of publication, Twitter was testing 280 characters.

The use of fast-paced multimedia has affected Pivotals' ability to focus and analyze complex information. As we've already mentioned, research conducted by Microsoft Corp. found the average attention span has decreased from 12 seconds to 8 seconds.[7]

But remember, teens use that eight-second attention span as a finely tuned filter to sort and digest content at lightning-fast speeds. Marketers, think light snacks in lieu of a steak dinner. Pivotals just don't have the time to digest anything heavy.

CASE STUDY

Who: Tasty

What: Buzzfeed's food brand, Tasty, creates the ultimate snackable content with its series of shareable, minute-long cooking videos.

How: Perfectly suited to Pivotals, Tasty's videos are captivating and snappy, leaving little room for boredom. Notorious for its time-lapse editing and aerial viewpoint, the videos appeal specifically to visually focused Gen Zers. Plus, it can't hurt that Gen Zers are known foodies who prefer delicious, high-quality options.[8]

Impact: In just over a year, Tasty had created 2,000 recipe videos that each reached 500 million people a month, generating nearly 1.8 billion views, primarily through Facebook.[9]

Emojis, Emoticons, and Stickers—Oh My!

By now, it's important to realize that phone calls and standard text-only messages are *so yesterday*. Today, Pivotals communicate speedily and visually. Enter emojis, emoticons, and stickers. (See Figure 3-3.)

EMOTICONS

A typographic display
of a facial representation,
used to convey emotion
in a text-only medium

EMOJIS

A small digital image or
icon used to express an
idea, emotion, etc., in
electronic communication

STICKERS

A detailed illustration of
a character that represents
an emotion or action

Figure 3-3 Emoticon, emoji, and sticker comparison.

"Believe it or not, emojis have been around for nearly 20 years," explains Megan Haines, founder and CEO of Karmies, which creates custom, interactive emojis. Shigetaka Kurita invented emojis in 1998 while working for DoCoMo, a large Japanese mobile communication company. He wanted to create a way for users to send pictures back and forth without using much data. The idea was simple: to "create a one character 'code' that would display as an icon on the other person's device."

Fast forward to today: We send emojis at a rate of more than six billion per day. Haines contends emojis allow for context. "In a world where text messaging has surpassed in-person communication and voice calls, we need a way to color that text and extract the full meaning of what's really being said," she explains. "Written words alone often times are too open to interpretation when it comes to the nuances of everyday communication."

Communicating through images and symbols isn't limited to Pivotals. Check your own Facebook feed or scroll through recent texts on your phone. Chances are you'll find emojis, emoticons, or stickers peppered throughout. In fact, Oxford Dictionaries made history in

2015 when they named "emoji" the Word of the Year for its popularity and heavy usage.

If you don't yet see how this matters to marketing, consider this: a Cisco Systems, Inc. report predicts 84 percent of all marketing communication will be visual by 2018.[10] The increase isn't exclusive to any particular medium, either. Visual communication is happening everywhere—newspapers, websites, social media, emails, and more. Ever wonder why Google changes its homepage logo daily, or why Ikea has no text in their furniture assembly instructions? Graphics are simple and span language barriers with ease. There are other benefits to visual communications as well. (See Figure 3-4).

"People are always finding creative new ways to use language," Haines noted. "As pop culture shifts and changes, so can the meaning of even the simplest emoji. For example, at one time the smiley face reminded people of the 'Rollback Prices' campaign Walmart used to feature, or the t-shirt scene from Forrest Gump."

However, Haines warns brands to consider the audience before incorporating emojis. Depending on location, age, and background, the classic unicode-based emojis may hold different meanings. *The Wall Street Journal* created a clever video that illustrates how six people from various walks of life interpreted the same emoji to mean entirely different things. One person thought two hands touching to mean "high five," while another thought it symbolized praying. One person saw a pink peach, and someone else saw someone's rear end. And that brown swirly thing with eyes? Is it chocolate ice cream, or ...?

While some companies are recognizing the popularity of emojis and devising ways to incorporate them into marketing efforts, it's important to tread lightly. As it turns out, emoji usage may not be a good approach for all brands or even for public figures.

Case in point: In an effort to appeal to young voters during the 2015 Democratic campaign, Hillary Clinton tweeted: "How does your student debt make you feel? Tell us in 3 emojis or less." One

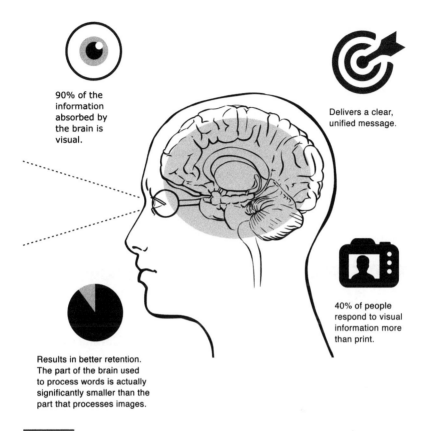

90% of the information absorbed by the brain is visual.

Delivers a clear, unified message.

40% of people respond to visual information more than print.

Results in better retention. The part of the brain used to process words is actually significantly smaller than the part that processes images.

Figure 3-4 Benefits of visual communications. [11, 12, 13]

Twitter user answered, "This is like when your mom tried to be hip in front of your friends and totally failed at it."

Of this notorious Clinton Twitter debacle, Haines says, "If the emoji usage isn't clever, or doesn't have an obvious need to be used—meaning why not just tweet it in 140 characters or less?—it can come off as trying too hard."

The message may seem especially inauthentic if the brand or figure isn't a typical emoji user, which was also the case for Clinton.

Despite the necessity of these watch-outs, Haines is excited about the future of emojis. With the development of platforms such as

Karmies, she sees new emojis reaching millions of smartphones in a matter of seconds to represent timely events:

> For example, as soon as it's decided which two teams are in the Super Bowl, or which two candidates are left on *The Bachelor*, we can release emojis that allow users to talk about their favorite on messaging apps or on social media. Even more interesting might be the data that comes from the use of these emojis to be able to tell which way the favorites are playing.

CASE STUDY

Who: Domino's Pizza

What: The brand created a permanent feature allowing customers to place pizza orders by simply tweeting the pizza emoji at Domino's: 🍕.

How: The campaign works by accessing consumers' Easy Order profile once they register their Twitter handle on Domino's website. Once Domino's receives the tweet, the customer receives a confirmation message for the order, and the pizza is made and sent to his or her home.

Impact: The pizza chain turned a mundane activity—ordering a pizza—into something novel and innovative. Since Domino's already receives half of its business through online orders, the option to "tweet-a-pizza" makes it even more convenient for those inclined to order digitally. The campaign received significant media coverage and won the Cannes Titanium Grand Prix for most breakthrough idea of the year in 2016.

CASE STUDY

Who: Dunkin' Donuts

What: Dunkin' Donuts became the first national coffee chain to allow gifting and payment within Apple's iMessage.

How: Customers can send the gift of coffee more easily than ever using Apple Pay on the Dunkin' Donuts app. The app also boasted its own set of original Dunkin' Donuts stickers that can be downloaded from Apple's App Store. Fans can also create virtual greeting cards with DD's iMessage Card Builder.

Impact: By embracing iMessage, Dunkin' Donuts committed to making its brand as accessible as possible. Apple Pay, already a popular in-store option, enabled customers to pay securely via mobile, while the stickers provided a new way for users to interact with the brand.

ALL THE VIDEOS:
THE YOUTUBE EFFECT

The YouTube Effect: The phenomenon in which you navigate to a single video hosted on YouTube, then find yourself clicking on related videos until you wake up hours later to find yourself watching Chocolate Rain for the umpteenth time or enjoying the musical stylings of Rick Astley.

—FROM THE URBAN DICTIONARY

Video content encompasses everything Pivotals love. It's right up there with oxygen, water, and food as essential to daily survival. If your goal is to target and engage the Pivotal generation, video is a must-have. Where do teens go for video? YouTube. It's the video equivalent of Google.

According to a 2016 report from DEFY Media, teens are on "watch" from sunup (65 percent report viewing before school or work) to sundown (67 percent watch while falling asleep), often without many breaks.[14]

Why do they love mobile video so much? For entertainment, sure. But it's much more than that. It's how they stay up to speed on what's current and culturally relevant. It's educational. It's a stress reliever. It's relatable (especially when it comes from social influencers that feel like friends). It keeps them connected with their peers.

Remember when we were teens and had to wait for hours, if not days, for our favorite MTV music video to air? Teens today are lucky. They can watch video anytime, anywhere (as we said, even at school).

They also tend to follow an unspoken standard of behavior. A recent survey from Sharethrough, a native advertising software firm, found that 87 percent of Pivotals watch video with the sound on and that 85 percent watch it in full-screen when they are home.[15] When at school, work, or commuting, however, they prefer to have the volume off.

What are the implications for brands and marketers? Where do we start?

First, marketers must think about how to engage Pivotals throughout the course of the day. Pivotals can and will consume video from almost anywhere and at almost every time of day. But the creative and visual implications of mobile video will require an original approach. We can't just put a TV commercial online and call it quits.

Second, marketers should consider the context of where they're posting the video. If teens are watching videos with the sound off, headlines and short descriptions will take on new importance. They can't be an afterthought because a great headline might make the difference between someone watching or skipping your video. Facebook videos now automatically display closed captions, as many people at work or on the go leave their sound off and read the captions so as not to be disruptive.

According to Chris Schreiber, vice president of marketing and communications at Sharethrough, 67 percent of Gen Z prefers reading the headline and description as the video plays on mute. Eighty-four percent said a headline determines whether or not they watch an infeed video ad.[16] Schreiber advises marketers to "think about corresponding elements and how a headline ties it together."

Third, marketers have a limited window to hook audiences. "We see instantaneous decision-making by Gen Z and younger generations who are mobile savvy," says Schreiber.[17]

While Pivotals will skip ads at nearly any cost, they *will* sit through ads they find entertaining. Teens like ads that give them the sense they are part of something bigger—part of a cultural movement. They also are much more attracted to ads that allow them to play a contributing role compared to older generations.[18] Music and humor are important, too, as well as a commercial's aesthetic qualities. And teens will pay attention to the use of innovation, like virtual reality (VR) and augmented reality (AR). (See Figure 3-5.)

"The gaming effect," or content that allows for a greater sense of participation, is another important consideration when creating videos. Teens spend an exorbitant amount of time playing video games and not just from the confines of their rooms. Remember, Pokémon Go had teens and their families out and about, exploring the real world on the hunt for virtual Pokémon creatures. That is participation media.

Video content must engage more than only the visual senses to be as captivating as gaming. Pivotals won't be content to sit back and watch pretty pictures. They want to feel as though they're part of the action. Incorporate gaming mechanics into your video content, such as voting, rewards, points, contests, and competition.

SMALL BUDGET

You don't need big bucks to produce the personable, engaging videos your audience desires. A small budget and a little creativity can take you a long way.

KNOW YOUR AUDIENCE

Know your audience's interests and values before creating video content for them. Looking at statistics within your demographic can be essential.

SMALL BITES

Keep it fresh by experimenting with varying types of content. More than half of 18- to 54-year-olds share videos on social media, so a well-crafted, snackable video focused on your product might be your secret to success.

A LITTLE CREATIVITY

A short video means telling a story in less than 30 seconds. It may be a challenge for a service that isn't instructional, but you still have the option to highlight sales, campaigns, and new merchandise.

Figure 3-5 Tips for creating compelling videos.[19]

Remember, videos are like air to this generation, so never end the supply. A one-and-done approach won't cut it. (See Figure 3-5 for tips on creating compelling videos.)

CONTENT STRATEGY

Today, mobile content is about engagement and discovery, not interruptive advertising. Companies must think of content as an opportunity for the brand's voice to fit into Pivotals' lives, however small the screen may be.

When asked how to create a Pivotal-focused mobile content strategy, Jake Katz, Revolt Mobile vice president of audience insights and strategy, recommended starting by humanizing your brand. This means giving the brand a personality that consumers can engage with. Consumers are ingesting content in the context of their daily lives, and marketers have to meet them there: in line at the grocery store, enjoying the outdoors, or relaxing with friends.[20]

So, marketers, don't sell. Rather, take a seat and join teens in their journey, one that should be complete with the following characteristics: authentic, fast, seamless, consistent, friendly, human, humorous, autonomous, compassionate, and secure.

Authentic

Teenagers hate when their parents try to act cool around their friends, and they feel the same about brands or public figures (sorry, Hillary) that try to act "hip" to get their attention. Amanda Gutterman, vice president of growth at digital media company Dose, says, "Gen Z isn't anti-corporate or anti-brand; they just have an amazing nose for B.S."[21]

While they trust brands less than previous generations did and will do everything in their power to skip traditional ads, Pivotals are open to engaging with brands—as long as it's on their terms. But their terms are pretty steep, which is perhaps why Pivotals engage less with brands overall than other generations do.

Fast

We've mentioned this before, but it's important enough to repeat: You only have eight seconds or less to capture Pivotals' attention. Don't waste valuable time! Secure attention fast with compelling, relevant content.

Consider everything we've been talking about in this chapter. Is it ideal for mobile? Do you have strong visuals? What about video? Are you sharing something of interest in the first three seconds? If they find you appealing, they will take the time to get to know more about you. If not, they will quickly move on. If you successfully capture their interest, they will do a deep-dive with your brand. If what you offer doesn't interest them, they won't linger to see what else you have to offer.

Seamless and Consistent

Pivotals expect a seamless experience across every screen and on every channel. The buzzword of the moment is "omnichannel." But that doesn't mean repurposing every piece of content across all platforms.

You can't simply put a 30-second TV commercial on Facebook or YouTube and call it a day. Your content needs to match the purpose of the channel on which it's shared. Snapchat is raw and mostly silly; Instagram is filtered and aspirational; Twitter is quippy and newsy. Operate within the context of the platform and follow its rules as defined by this generation.

Friendly

Be personable. Have authentic, two-way conversations with Pivotals, both online and offline. Your in-store customer service should mirror your mobile experience. If a brand is quick to respond to a tweet with a fun comment but its in-store experience is uptight and stiff, it has lost its chance at a lasting friendship.

The idea of brand loyalty isn't automatic for Pivotals; brands must earn the relationship. As a brand, your interactions reflect what's important to consumers. Recognize their passions, interests, and values, as well as the type of content they seek.

Human

Consumers trust people more than brands, and this is no different with Pivotals. They want to be treated like people, not numbers, and expect their favorite brands to act accordingly. How do you humanize your brand?

Just like the human experience, there is no one-size-fits-all solution.

Do be sure to show your brand's personality by building an engaging narrative and backstory. Create an emotional bond with your customers, and listen to what they have to say—it shows you care. Own up to your mistakes, but don't be too serious. Simply put, a faceless brand will get lost in the crowd. It's important to be accessible, interesting, and relatable.

Don't let overthinking stunt your creative process. While it is increasingly more difficult for a brand to buy its way into consumers' minds, targeting your demographic requires authenticity and an insider's perspective.

According to Katz, having an influencer is the key to building an audience among the variety of platforms available: "The content marketing experts of our time are not brands," claims Katz. "Social media stars naturally understand how to build, retain, and engage an audience in new media more than any big name in marketing." (More on this in Chapter 4.)

Humorous

Don't know what's funny to Pivotals? Just ask! Get a group of Pivotals together, and have them show you the top five funniest videos on YouTube right now. What they share may catch you off guard. As explained in Chapter 2, they have an offbeat, quirky, often raw, and even self-deprecating sense of humor. To most of us adults, it might seem downright absurd. But hey, who are we to argue? The consumer is always right.

Autonomous

Don't force them to watch your videos. They demand control over the ad experience. If they see a video they can't skip, they'll probably look away. In fact, it's better to give them some control. According to a multicountry report by global research agency Kantar Millward Brown, 59 percent of Gen Zers prefer mobile reward video ads (e.g., the videos they control) versus the 15 percent who prefer nonskippable.[22]

While Millennials aren't far behind on this trend, it's clear Pivotals desire more control over their ad experience than any generation before. Pivotals are easily distracted or annoyed, leading to more than 50 percent installing mobile ad-blockers in protest. So, odds are, if they aren't in control, they aren't watching. Marketers, reward your audience for engaging with your ads or at the very least let them drive.

Compassionate

Pivotals recognize their privilege in having such advanced technology and seek out opportunities to use their access to help others. Brands should aid them in their efforts to support the issues that are at the core of what matters to them today.

According to a sparks & honey report, 26 percent of 16- to 19-year-olds are active volunteers,[23] 60 percent want to change the world using their careers, and 76 percent worry about the environmental impact humans are having on the Earth.[24] Our research also indicated that human equality is the defining issue Gen Z rallies behind, specifically racial and LGBTQ rights.

A great example of engaging the compassionate generation is Verizon with its HopeLine campaign.[25] Mobile phone users can donate used and functional phones to HopeLine, which then distributes the proceeds to domestic violence victims. It also serves a double purpose as it protects the environment from improper tech disposal. Through a single campaign, Verizon helped people in need, lessened harm to the environment, and enabled the socially conscious to join in.

Marketers trying to connect with Pivotals should project their philanthropic side and be sure to demonstrate—not just talk about—the brand's commitment to a cause.

Secure

To deliver highly personalized and relevant content, marketers have begun to lean on data more than ever before. Collecting locations, behavior, and clicks "behind the scenes" has become a common practice to enhance the Pivotal experience.

Because of this, it's important to note Pivotals do expect privacy, honesty, and integrity any time personal information is collected. Pivotals have high standards of security and expect marketers to comply. Brands should always disclose what data they will collect, how long it will be held, and for what purpose it will be used. This very vocal and uniquely private group will not tolerate a breach of trust.

WHAT IT ALL MEANS

Marketers, close your laptops. Put away your books (except this one, of course). Take a minute to relax and look around. Gen Z is communicating faster than you can plan, learning faster than you can teach, and consuming faster than you can create. So take a deep breath and stop trying to get it perfect. Instead, just get real.

First, when planning your content strategy for Pivotals, consider the context of where your message will appear. Ask yourself: Where can we eliminate redundancy? Can the title of the video serve a higher purpose? How long does this ad *really* need to be? Who's sharing this post? What does this say about our brand?

Second, take a step back and look at the whole picture. If your message isn't clear within that eight-second window, see what you can cut down, clear up, or optimize. How does this page look on an iPhone? Will this translate to desktop? Where will the audience be when watching this? Will they need sound?

It's tempting to want to overexplain your value proposition and, honestly, rather strange not to have a lengthy product description. Pivotals are moving fast, however, and if you don't pick up speed, you'll never catch them. Speak their language and get visual. If a picture is worth a thousand words, then you have all the time you need.

KEY TAKEAWAYS

- **Pivotals aren't mobile-*first*, they're mobile-*only*.** What marketers used to call the "third screen," the mobile phone, is Pivotals' first—and in many cases, *only*—screen.

- **Pivotals are conditioned to handle mass amounts of visual stimuli.** Studies even suggest their brains have evolved to process more information at faster speeds.

- **Brands must optimize for the smaller screen from the ground up if they expect to appeal to younger consumers.** Websites originally designed for the mobile user are called "mobile-first" with desktop as a secondary concern.

- **Pivotals can and will consume video from almost anywhere, at almost every time of day.** It's how they stay up to speed on what's current, and it keeps them connected with their peers.

- **They want to be treated like people, not numbers, and expect their favorite brands to act accordingly.** Show your brand's personality by building an engaging narrative and creating an emotional bond with your consumers.

A MATTER OF INFLUENCE

magine you're back in high school, walking down the hall between classes. You pass a group of popular kids who happen to all be wearing Nike sweatpants. You overhear one of them casually mention how many pairs they have stocked up at home. You take mental note, and the next time you go shopping, you beg your mom to splurge on a pair of beautiful black Nike joggers. They're expensive, sure, but it's a price worth paying to up your "cool" game.

Fast-forward to today, when influential teens or groups of teens don't just roam the halls of high schools or universities. They reside online, projecting their influence to the masses—anytime, anywhere. Savvy marketers are tapping into this influence to reach and engage with Pivotals through the channels they use most.

Not only are Pivotals influencing one another, but they carry powerful clout over their parents and families' buying habits. Due to the sheer amount of information they can take in and process at a moment's notice, Pivotals often possess more knowledge about brands and products than their parents. As a result, the dynamic and structure of the traditional family unit is changing.

Unlike the Millennial generation before them, Pivotals are more resistant and less receptive to traditional advertising. In fact, they don't want to be "advertised to" at all. They're not antibrand. They just hate anything that feels invasive or forced. Marketers need to know how to tap into the power of influence—through the right *influencers*—to get and keep Pivotals' attention.

WHAT IS INFLUENCE?

Influence is an invisible—yet powerful—force that can't be denied. It impacts our choices every day, from where we go for lunch to what shoes we buy. Whether we realize it or not, influence played a role in our final decision.

—JOSEPH COLE, VP OF MARKETING AT TAPINFLUENCE, A
LEADING INFLUENCER MARKETING
AUTOMATION SOLUTION

Maslow's Hierarchy of Needs

In the 1940s, Abraham Maslow developed the hierarchy of needs model to help us better understand human motivation. He probably didn't intend this as a marketing playbook for the next century, but nonetheless marketers still use this pyramid to help target ads toward consumer needs at different levels of the hierarchy. (See Figure 4-1.)

After all, brands connect best with prospective customers when they can appeal to their needs in a relevant, meaningful way.[1] For example, consider stage two of Maslow's hierarchy. New parents who are mostly concerned about the safety of their infant might be most receptive to car ads that focus on safety features.

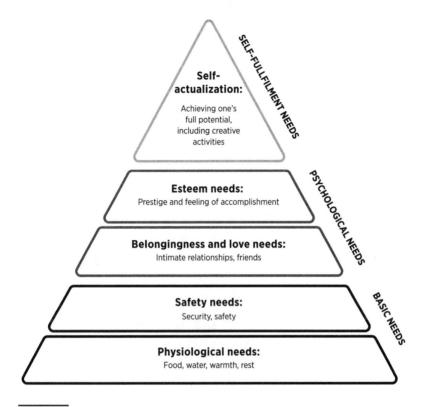

Figure 4-1 Maslow's hierarchy of needs.

But let's not stop at Maslow. A chapter about influence wouldn't be complete without Dale Carnegie. In his 1936 book *How to Win Friends and Influence People*, Carnegie establishes 12 key ways to win over people to your way of thinking, many of which still apply today. Carnegie encourages beginning conversations in a friendly way, being sympathetic, and putting yourself in the other person's shoes.

As marketing shifts to a more relationship-centric approach with consumers and digital content becomes king, Carnegie's principles are just as relevant today as they were in 1936.

Because clever marketing tricks and gimmicks don't fool Pivotals, building authentic relationships with them is key. Pivotals expect brands to know them and deliver highly personalized messaging. To be honest. To be sympathetic. And, yes, to even treat them like friends.

Influence at Home

There has never been a generation with more influence both inside and outside the family . . . Seventy-eight percent of parents with children in this group feel that their kids are more involved in their family's decisions than they themselves were as children.

—ZENO GROUP[2]

When you were a teenager, you probably didn't have much say about what type of TV your parents bought, where your family spent summer vacations, or even what your mom made for dinner. In fact, if you were brave enough to speak up, you likely were met with a response like "You'll eat what I put on the table, and you'll like it!" Or, better yet, the age-old parental rebuttal to every unwelcome question: "Because I said so!"

For thousands of years, the balance of power in families has been hierarchical, with parents making most, if not all major decisions. But that's no longer the case. For many reasons—including the changing structure of the traditional family and teens' increased access to information—we have moved from a hierarchy to a democracy regarding family decision making.[3]

Changing Family Structure

The average family as we once knew it—a mother, father, and 2.5 children—has since been replaced by a diverse collection of single-parent, unmarried/cohabiting partners, and reconstructed families. In 1960, 37 percent of households included a married couple raising their own children. Today, only 16 percent of households resemble the traditional nuclear family.[4]

Americans are also delaying marriage, waiting longer to have children, and having fewer children. Additionally, more babies are born to unmarried mothers than ever before, and U.S. Census data shows that in 2015, 16 percent of single parents were dads. In fact, dads are carrying the full parenting load in more families than ever before.

In single-parent or dual-income households, parents have less time. They have no choice but to rely on their children for input into household decisions and purchases. Given that kids and teens have 24/7 access to information and a natural inclination to learn and explore, most parents happily delegate product research to their offspring.

For instance, ask Pivotals to consider family-friendly vacation spots, and they're likely to come back with a comprehensive list, perhaps even a PowerPoint presentation with corresponding visuals of well-researched choices. And if they have a personal favorite, they'll employ expert bargaining and persuasion tactics to "sell" their choice. Pivotals know their market, they've done their research; for all intents and purposes, they are master negotiators.

This means Pivotals are primed to succeed as family roles and communication become more open and democratic. Moms aren't the only ones buying groceries and household items. Dads aren't the only ones buying cars and electronics. Kids today understand the value of money, and as their parents see this understanding in practice, kids and teens will take on even more responsibility.

With $44 billion of their own money to spend, and potentially influencing more than $665 billion in family spending, Pivotals are a formidable market with intense buying power.

Influencing Family Decisions

A recent YouGov Omnibus Parents Survey examining kids' influence on their parents' buying decisions shows that children are "active decision makers in family economies." However, the degree of influence varies based on the type of purchase.[5] (See Figure 4-2.)

The survey analyzed kids' influence across a range of categories and a range of ages, as the opinions and persuasive power of young kids often rival those of teens. Looking at categories in which adults do the purchasing, the report shows Pivotals are most likely to have at least some degree of input into adult purchases.

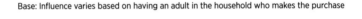

Base: Influence varies based on having an adult in the household who makes the purchase

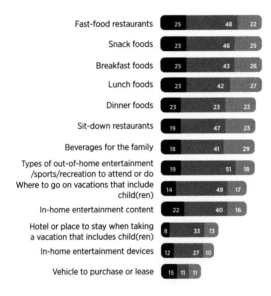

● Child picks independently   ● Child shares opinions;   ● Child's likes and dislikes are already
   or with parent.   these influence the purchase.   known; these influence purchase.

Figure 4-2   Kids' role in household purchasing and shopping decisions.[6]

Dining options tend to be the areas where Pivotals exert the most influence. A quarter of Gen Zers pick the fast-food restaurants and breakfast foods for their families, followed closely by snack foods and lunch foods.

Kids have the second highest influence on their parents regarding family recreational activities. Half of all parents are influenced by their children's opinions in choosing out-of-home entertainment and family vacation destinations.

Pester Power

But when shopping together, all bets are off! In fact, with kids in tow, mothers will spend up to 30 percent more.[7] Never underestimate the "pester power" of kids and teens: They are expert verbal negotiators, often promising to get better grades or do additional chores around the house, sometimes even offering to pay for part of the purchase themselves.

In the same YouGov survey, 42 percent of parents said they have buckled under the pressure of their child's attempt to get them to buy a particular product.

Of course, it's not just the Pivotals doing the influencing. Teens are just as heavily influenced by their parents. As mentioned in Chapter 1, Pivotals' most important role models are their caregivers. Per Youth-Beat Total Year 2016 data, 50 percent of parents say their parenting style is similar to how their own parents raised them, including the ways they involve their children in purchase decisions.[8] While it's natural for teens to want to push back on parental involvement as they grow older, teens today are more accepting of their parents' input, especially regarding money matters. Pivotals grew up watching their parents and families struggle financially and, through those experiences, have grown into discerning customers.

"Our research shows that parents remain the strongest influence on the money habits their children develop and practice as adults," said Andrew Plepler with Bank of America in a 2015 press release.

But for as much influence as their parents may have, Pivotals' peers are the most influential when it comes to buying decisions.

Influence on the Outside

Being liked by our peers is a fundamental need for every generation of teens. Even with social media, Pivotals today are still influenced more by their real-life friends than by anyone else. The only difference is that this validation comes from sources outside one's immediate circle of friends, and it's given almost constantly via social media.

"Peer pressure is the internalization of unspoken, external norms or expectations received by an individual from their peer group," said Dr. Ken Sonnenschein, a child and adolescent psychiatrist. He went on:

> I don't think peer pressure is better or worse due to social media. However, I do think social media as a phenomenon has sped up the process and allowed exposure to an internationalization of a much wider group of norms and expectations. The game is the same but the field is much larger and the ball is moving much faster.

Eighty-nine percent of Pivotals said they would be more likely to enter a store based on where their friends shop. Those friends, according to 62 percent of Pivotals, are the most influential factor in their buying decisions. Only 14 percent cited athletes as the most influential factor on buying decisions, and bloggers/YouTubers followed closely at 13 percent. Celebrity and singer endorsements were ranked as the lowest influence at just 6 and 7 percent, respectively.[9]

A recent study published in *Psychological Science* proves social media "likes" actually impact teens' brains and behaviors.[10] The experiment, conducted at UCLA, used a photo-sharing app similar to Instagram to display 148 photographs, 40 of which were submitted by the participating teenagers. Every photo displayed the number of likes it had received from the other participants, though in actuality the researchers had predetermined these numbers.

When participants saw that their own photos had received a large number of likes, their nucleus accumbens—the part of the brain's reward circuitry—lit up with activity. This reward circuitry is most responsive during adolescence. In fact, for teenagers, acquiring a high number of likes on a status or photo activates "the same brain circuits that are activated by eating chocolate and winning money." Additionally, the social brain and visual attention regions of the brain showed strong activation upon viewing a high number of likes on one's own photo.

The effects of peer influence in social media were also evident, as teens tended to like the photos that had markedly more likes versus the ones with only a few likes.

"We showed the same photo with a lot of likes to half of the teens and to the other half with just a few likes," said lead author Lauren Sherman. "Teens react differently to information when they believe it has been endorsed by many or few of their peers, even if these peers are strangers."[11]

YouthBeat refers to this as the "American Idol" effect. That show introduced the concept of crowdsourcing to a generation of young people, revolutionizing the path to fame/popularity.

Of course, peer influence extends well beyond simple likes in social media.

By sharing their unique perspectives and opinions across YouTube, Instagram, Twitter, Snapchat, Musical.ly, and more, the most influential Pivotal trendsetters are developing real relationships with their followers, based on engagement and trust. In return, they are building passionate, informed, and in some cases brand-focused followers.

And tapping into those close-knit, trusted communities of passionate followers is the Holy Grail for marketers.

INFLUENCER MARKETING

With brands making an average of $6 for every $1 spent on influencer marketing, it's no wonder this is one of the fastest-growing ways to connect with consumers on social.

—*ADWEEK*, 2015

In 2012, Brian Solis wrote *The Rise of Digital Influence*, a how-to guide for businesses to spark desirable effects and outcomes through social media influence. Then, in 2015, *Adweek* called it the "Next Big Thing" in marketing, saying it would open a new channel for brands to connect with consumers more directly, organically, and at scale.[12] Today, influencer marketing has grown into one of the hottest trends in social media, and it's living up to the hype as a proven channel delivering real results.

But influencer marketing is nothing new. Since the dawn of advertising, businesses and brands have tapped into people with influence—typically celebrities and well-known public figures—to promote products and services. Joan Crawford and Pepsi. Brooke Shields and Calvin Klein Jeans. Michael Jordan and Nike. The list goes on.

Today, however, due to the emergence of social media platforms, celebrities no longer have a monopoly on influence. "Regular" people are gaining influence online based on their unique voice, opinion, or expertise. This has widened the playing field for marketers looking to tap into people with influence to help promote their brand or product.

Since blogs first came on the scene in the early 2000s, marketers have been trying to figure out how to leverage them for brand benefit. This became especially prevalent when "mommy bloggers" started documenting the trials and tribulations of parenting, using their blogs to educate and inspire one another. What's more, these authentic conversations about motherhood led to sharing advice, opinions, and product recommendations.

This makes sense, since moms have always been more receptive to word-of-mouth marketing than men or even other non-mom females. Blogs merely gave them a new way to engage in conversations around brands and products.

Blogs were just the beginning. Today, online influence comes from nearly every corner of the social media landscape. Facebook. YouTube. Instagram. Twitter. Snapchat. Musical.ly. Name a social platform, and you'll find individuals or groups who have built meaningful relationships with their followers. Influencers gain followers by creating human connections and building trust with their audiences. Because people trust other people more than they trust brands, marketers recognize the unique opportunity that influencer marketing provides.

The Perfect Storm

If influencer marketing is nothing new, and if blogs and social media have been around for a decade or more, why is it garnering so much attention now? Tapinfluence, a leading influencer-marketing automation provider, outlined some major shifts for marketers, influencers, and consumers that have created the "perfect storm" for influencer marketing today.[13]

Marketers

For marketers, the shifts require a broader grasp of messaging and a deeper understanding of data. The famous quote from John Wanamaker, "Half the money I spend on advertising is *wasted*; the trouble is I don't know which half," *no longer applies.* The shift to digital marketing has placed a heavy emphasis on data. Nearly every effort can be tracked, measured, and attributed, meaning no sale goes uncredited.

This focus on data extends to social circles as well, thanks to the beauty of social media. Software is popping up all over the place, offering so-called Return on Sentiment, analysis, and word-of-mouth analytics. Pivotals pick the social channel, and marketers must follow, leaving digital bread crumbs wherever they go.

Similarly, the content that marketers measure has shifted dramatically from "Here's how awesome our product is!" to the customers themselves controlling the narrative. From reviews to tweets, the brands must present a relatable message and encourage a positive conversation. But at the end of the day, regardless of tracking and effort, Pivotals own the story.

Influencers

Influencers also have had to shift their content toward short-form, visually centric platforms like Pinterest, Instagram, and Snapchat in order to retain audience engagement and interaction. Though long-form content, like blogs, once dominated, influencers on visual platforms tend to make more money through sponsored content.

Not only has influencer content changed, but target demographics have as well. Millennials and Pivotals are now the targets for branded content, with influencers spanning every age range. What's most important is that influencers produce engaging, authentic content, and the way to do it is to integrate them into the campaign's creative process early on.

With such an increase in the dedication, quality, and visibility of the influencer, it's no wonder many of them are able to transition their passions into full-time, paid careers. Pivotals even see becoming an influencer as a viable, attainable career option.

Consumers

Consumers, over time, have come to see peers as more credible than brands, even if the content is sponsored. As long as the content holds value as genuine, educational, or entertaining, consumers will still engage with it.

The key is having authentic and meaningful content, as Pivotals are distrustful of traditional advertising that tries to "trick" them. Especially in an age of auto-play videos, pop-ups, and pre-roll ads, an advertisement must be credible.

Finally, Pivotals expect easy access to content via mobile. Smartphones are the primary online interface, and users want the ability to connect when their timeline allows.

The "New" Celebrities

We're no longer as easily swayed by celebrities sequestered in their mansions, famous for being famous. We like influencers who feel more relatable, who will talk to us on social media and like our comments on their YouTube post—we like that they feel like one of us.

—GRACE MASBACK

If you're still banking on the Beyoncés, Taylor Swifts, and Justin Biebers of the world to blast your message to young consumers, you're wasting both time and money.

Collaborating with social influencers and content creators in their respective channels of prominence has overtaken the traditional celebrity endorsement. Brands benefit from the halo of trust and authenticity offered by "real people" sharing "real" content with their fans and followers.

In the 2015 Cassandra Report by digital agency Deep Focus, 63 percent of respondents from Generation Z reported they would rather be marketed to by "real people" than by celebrities.[14] And according to a recent *Variety* poll, 8 out of the 10 most "approachable, authentic and influential" people for teen audiences are YouTube stars.[15]

With the rise of social media influencers to near "star status," how do we tell the difference, and how do marketers decide which influencers are worth their investment? What's more, if the old advertising rules don't apply, how do you work with them on behalf of your brand?

The New Rules of Engagement

Traditionally, celebrities become famous through their involvement in film, television, fashion, music, or sports. They gain admiration based primarily on talent. Celebrity endorsement is a way to harness a celebrity's popularity and associate a brand or product with it to increase brand recognition and value.

Social media influencers, on the other hand, have risen to "fame" simply by being themselves (or hyperexaggerated versions of themselves). They have built homegrown communities of followers based on shared interests and ideas and have earned the admiration of their followers based on a sense of friendship and trust. In fact, Think with Google describes the Pivotal relationship with social media influencers as "friendship," in lieu of "fanship."[16] Some of the most popular influencer industries are fashion/beauty, gaming, travel, food, home, and fitness.

By tapping into trusted social media influencers, brands can create word-of-mouth marketing that feels like it's coming from a friend rather than someone paid to represent the brand. Even though influencers are, in fact, often paid by the brands they endorse, most work only with brands that align with their authentic voice and topic of expertise. Their fans and followers trust that they won't "sell out" to brands that don't align with their personal values.

However, Forrester analyst Jessica Liu warns that influencers have more in common with celebrity endorsers than the public believes. She says consumers must be savvy to "navigate the tricky gray area between authentic recommendation and paid endorsement." Since influencers often have no prior relationship with the brand, they might be inclined to endorse a product to gain recognition and money rather than because they genuinely believe the product is the best on the market. Liu goes on:

> Influencer marketing has evolved into just another paid channel. It's no different than a TV spot or print ad. However, Gen Z doesn't necessarily care. For them, it's more about their perceived connection with the influencer, and they don't care if that person is being paid to promote a brand or not. They're still more likely to listen.[17]

In some cases, there are gray areas between what constitutes a celebrity versus a social media influencer. Case in point: the Kardashians. While they rose to fame due to their reality television show, *Keeping Up with the Kardashians*, they have evolved that fame into social media mega-stardom. While the world might see Kim as the most famous Kardashian, Pivotals relate more to Kylie Jenner, Kim's younger, fashionista half-sister.

At first, you might wonder how a generation that wants to see "real" people can be attracted to Jenner. But behind her constantly changing, heavily made-up exterior, remember what Kylie (and the Kardashians) bring to the table:

▶ **Positive body image.** Due almost singlehandedly to the Kardashians, curves are cool again!

▶ **Entrepreneurship.** Kylie's cosmetics line, particularly her lip kits, regularly sell out worldwide.

▶ **Love of family.** They have one another's backs, no matter what!

▶ **Forward-thinking attitudes.** Their father, formerly known as Bruce Jenner, is now Caitlyn Jenner, an advocate for transgender people everywhere.

In the eyes of the Gen Z public, the Kardashians are compassionate people willing to share their struggles and fight for causes that most Pivotals believe in.

WHAT IT ALL MEANS

Here's the million-dollar question: How do brands work with social influencers to engage with Pivotals through relevant, compelling content?

In an Inc.com article, "10 Tips for Working with Social Media Influencers," author Joseph Steinberg shared the best ways to collaborate with influencers based on input from entrepreneur, investor, and business advisor Murray Newlands.

Newlands suggests engaging and making connections with influencers to foster positive, mutually beneficial relationships. "Influencers have choices among many great products, and will typically promote offerings of people and businesses that they know," he shares. Doing your research, making standout networking attempts, and being reputable are all important in getting a blogger to respond to a pitch.[18]

It's also important not only to let influencers take the wheel but to target influencers who love your product and embody the brand's values.

"Come up with an ideal list [of influencers] and then pitch those people based on what you know about the client and the campaign," advises Stephanie Funk, founder of social influence company Acorn. Influencers who do not fit with the brand will be unsuccessful in promoting it.

Even though influencers are paid, the product should be something they want to use. According to Newlands, there is more for influencers to gain than just money: Credibility, invitations to networking events, and products are all additionally attractive compensation.[19]

However, Funk says the life span of an influencer is comparable to that of a fly, so marketers should continually seek new influencers. As keeping up a blog is hard work, you cannot get too attached to particular influencers. Bloggers generally fade out of the spotlight within an average of three years.

With Pivotals, not all influencers require an enormous following. In fact, so-called micro influencers who have a small but loyal following are gaining traction with brands. Funk says they are "well-respected within the target market" and are seen more as friends than as celebrities, making these influencers preferable to a "huge reach of casually-connected fans." In addition, they are also usually much more affordable than more well-known influencers.

Funk agrees that consumers are open to messages from influencers that fit with the product. "When relevant influencers post about something to their seemingly online friends, those people are ready to receive those messages because they make sense."

Influencers are the experts when it comes to their audience; give them control when it comes to creativity. "Paying an influencer to simply share your content won't lead to the result you desire," says Newlands. "Give creative license to the influencer so he or she can introduce your brand authentically." The human element is what makes influencer advertising so effective, so playing that up is key.

The hunt for influencers can be a grueling process, so utilize the full span of the relationship. Newlands proposes using them as "reporters" for product releases and upcoming events with updates sent to their followers through social media. Sponsoring product giveaways, user-generated content contests, and sharing campaigns on the influencers' channel are other ways to create hype. "Make your campaign something memorable by engaging your influencer as the contest ringmaster," advises Newlands.[20]

CASE STUDY

Who: Truth

What: The antismoking nonprofit set out to create a video that, in an emotionally impactful way, would make it clear that smoking is not glamorous.

How: With the help of popular YouTubers such as Grace Helbig, Epic Meal Time's Harley Mortenstein, and AlphaCat, the brand created a song called "Left Swipe Dat," referencing Tinder's left swipe rejection feature to demonstrate not only that smoking is unattractive but that smokers get twice as many left swipes as nonsmokers. Along with a variety of comedians, musicians, and influencers, "Left Swipe Dat" features outrageous graphics that include a man on a dolphin riding a rainbow. The music video premiered during the 57th Annual Grammy Awards.

Impact: When the influencers shared their video, #LeftSwipeDat rose to the top of the worldwide trending topics. (See Figure 4-3.) The YouTubers, with more than 34.54 million followers between them, reached a massive target audience in a way that gave the message an authentic, relatable quality. Truth received the Cannes Bronze Lion Award for the campaign.

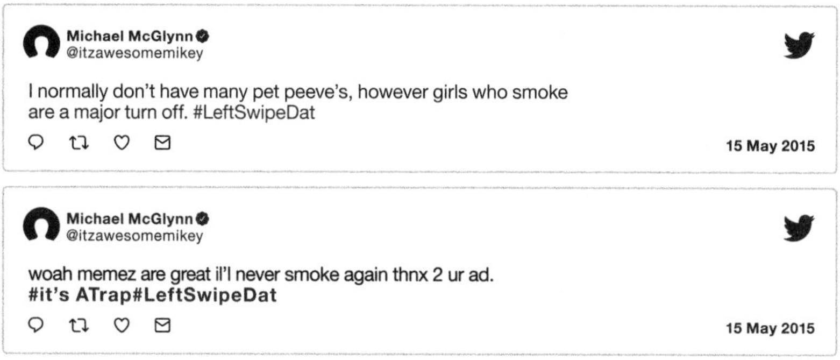

Michael McGlynn ✓
@itzawesomemikey

I normally don't have many pet peeve's, however girls who smoke
are a major turn off. #LeftSwipeDat

♡ ⇄ ♡ ✉   15 May 2015

Michael McGlynn ✓
@itzawesomemikey

woah memez are great il'l never smoke again thnx 2 ur ad.
#it's ATrap#LeftSwipeDat

♡ ⇄ ♡ ✉   15 May 2015

Figure 4-3   Rendering of Twitter responses to #LeftSwipeDat campaign.

The Fine Print

A final yet very important note about working with influencers: The
Federal Trade Commission (FTC) is paying close attention and doesn't
mess around when brands and influencers don't adhere to its strict
disclosure rules. If there is a material or incentivized connection between a brand and an influencer (money, gift, trade for free product,
family connection, or otherwise), that connection must clearly be dis-
closed on both sides.

In the past, influencers used hashtags like #sp, #ad, or #spon to
disclose an incentivized relationship with a brand. Today, that may
not be sufficient, per FTC's Endorsement Guides for deceptive advertising. The FTC is cracking down on brands when proper disclosures
are lacking. Companies like Lord & Taylor and Warner Bros. had to
learn the hard way. Violations can carry stiff fines.

To be safe, remain compliant. Always require that your influencers
clearly disclose any incentivized relationship. Include disclosure guidelines in your contracts with influencers, and pay close attention that
influencers adhere to your rules. After all, sanctions are likely to hit
brands harder than influencers.

The FTC regularly updates its Endorsement Guides. Make sure
you or your team is properly educated on the most recent guidelines
before you enter into influencer relationships.

KEY TAKEAWAYS

- **Not only do Pivotals influence one another, they also carry powerful clout over their parents and families' buying habits.** Teens often have more knowledge about brands and products than their parents. As a result, the dynamic and structure of the traditional family unit are changing.

- **Teens are just as heavily influenced by their parents.** Teens today are more accepting of their parents' input, especially regarding money matters. Pivotals grew up watching their parents and families struggle financially and, through those experiences, have grown into discerning customers.

- **Marketing tricks and gimmicks don't fool Pivotals.** Instead, build authentic relationships with them. Pivotals expect brands to know them and to deliver highly personalized messaging.

- **Brands benefit from the halo of trust and authenticity offered by "real people" sharing "real" content with their fans and followers.** Generation Z would rather be marketed to by "real people" than celebrities, and eight out of the 10 most "approachable, authentic, and influential" people for teen audiences are YouTube stars.

- **Clearly disclose all paid or incentivized relationships with social media influencers.** The FTC is cracking down on brands when proper disclosures are lacking. Violations can carry stiff fines.

BRAND ME

[Gen Z] are natural brand managers ... able to expertly manage
their personal and professional brands online to help them both fit
in and stand out the right amount.

—KRISTIE WONG, "GENERATION Z—WHO ARE THEY?"[1]

Sorry **Nike, Apple, Starbucks, Google** and, well . . . every other brand
on the planet. No matter how hard you try, you'll never be the
Pivotal generation's most beloved brand. That coveted spot is occu-
pied by the most significant brand of all: *ME.*

Don't misunderstand. Brand Me isn't exactly a narcissistic characteristic reminiscent of the selfie generation. It's more that the Pivotal
generation seeks to be understood and seen. First impressions take on
a new meaning for this generation as their physical appearance extends beyond wearing cool clothes. They now have an image to manage online. Their identity must be carefully curated to fully represent
who they believe they are. "Self" is created with intention.

Yet they realize on an intellectual level how "self" evolves over time.
They are a growth generation, open to new experiences and ideas, and
their unfolding personal brand is the best way to show the world they
are unique, authentic, and praiseworthy, regardless of their stage of life.

What does this mean for marketers? Everything! Media is not just a portal by which to deliver ads and promote your brand. That singular way of thinking is why so many brands are failing.

Today, Pivotals are looking to brands to improve what they see in themselves. The role for marketers is to partner with Pivotals on their journey to discover Brand Me.

BELONGING AS INDIVIDUALS

One of the key findings of our research was that being seen as unique is crucial to Pivotals. In fact, when asked how they want others to view them, nearly one-third of teens told us they would rather be considered *unique* than *real*. (See Figure 5-1.)

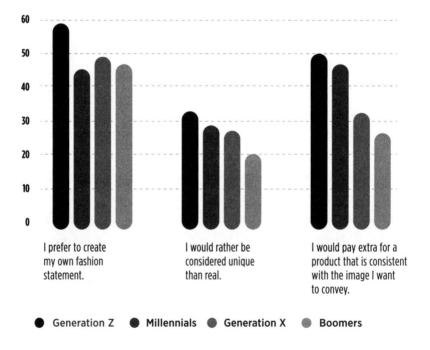

Figure 5-1 Uniqueness beliefs by generation.[2]

But that's not to say they want to be so unique they don't fit in. Remember, the whole goal of personal branding is to feel a sense of belonging. Like the generations of teens before, Pivotals seek validation and acceptance from their peers. Thus, Pivotals must create a persona that toes the line between different and relatable. To put in effort but not to try *too* hard.

Time-consuming? Absolutely. Teens spend countless hours crafting a version of themselves that is both different, alluring, and idealistic, while never straying from the beliefs, standards, and expectations of their peer group. What if they belong to multiple peer groups? The expectations double. A football player who enjoys jazz band? In that case, curating a personal brand requires creating *multiple* personas, all designed to appeal to the particular peer group. Oh, yeah, and the personas can't conflict too much because authenticity is still a concern.

If this sounds exhausting, it's because it is.

SELF-IMAGE AND THE PURSUIT OF PERFECTION

High school is tough. It's always been a popularity contest of sorts, but social media has amplified that pressure with a digital megaphone. A bad fashion choice doesn't just haunt teens as they walk the hallway. Their choices can follow them everywhere. The judgment and criticism don't stop when they get home. Nearly anyone can cultivate a personal image that's as public as a celebrity's or as influential as a brand's, whether they want to or not.

As a result, Pivotals obsess more over their appearance—offline *and* online—than generations past. With their curated identities so public, teens are hyperconscious of the way they present themselves.

A recent study by The Center for Generational Kinetics found 42 percent of Pivotals believe social media affects how people see you, and the same percentage say social media affects how you judge yourself.[3] This is five percentage points higher than Millennials, the original users of social media.

With stars like Ariana Grande refusing to pose on her "bad side" and Kylie Jenner receiving overwhelming media attention after rumors of cosmetic surgery at the age of 17, how can we expect teenagers to be immune to this preoccupation with image? When cultivating an audience to gain acceptance is the ultimate goal, Pivotals are guaranteed to take note of how the successful achieve and maintain their success, and, admittedly, self-image plays an important role.

A Common Sense Media survey called "Children, Teens, Media, and Body Image" found that girls are especially susceptible to concerns about their online personas:

▶ Thirty-five percent are worried about people tagging them in unattractive photos.
▶ Twenty-seven percent feel stressed about how they look in posted photos.
▶ Twenty-two percent felt bad about themselves if their photos were ignored.[4]

"Teens are their own eagle-eyed editors, programming content, limiting the volume of posts and paying close attention to quality content," said Nick Reggars, director of content strategy for Heat.[5]

This level of pressure on curation at such a young age has had a significant impact on this generation's self-esteem, and it's a direct result of being in the public eye during their formative years. According to a survey by the American Psychological Association, nearly one-third of U.S. teen girls feel bad when comparing themselves with others they see on social media, and other studies have found links between social media usage and low self-esteem.[6]

This issue, however, isn't unique to girls. British advertising think tank Credos sponsored a 2016 survey in which more than half of young male respondents cited social media, over even celebrities or advertising, as a source of pressure to look more attractive.[7]

These findings point to a self-conscious and hyperanalytical generation. They're watching the world around them, taking notes, and creating the best possible version of themselves to sell. They're the original brand managers.

MY CURATED SELF

We usually only present the best versions of ourselves on [social media], and leave the rest up to the imagination of the viewer.

—KATE DWYER, "WHY SOME OF SOCIAL MEDIA'S BIGGEST
STARS ARE DELETING THEIR ACCOUNTS—
AND MAYBE YOU SHOULD, TOO"[8]

Pivotals do not believe in a coming-of-age narrative. They view their brand identity not as a revelation occurring at a life milestone, such as starting a family or traveling abroad, but as a curated composition. That composition starts at a young age and is constantly evolving. Success isn't marked only by achievements but also by expression. Recognizing their true selves is far more important than celebrating their acceptance into adulthood. Which makes sense because, for this generation, categories, like adulthood, are irrelevant and fail to represent their daily evolution and discovery.

Whether through their Instagram feeds, gender expressions, or achievements, teens can decide who they want to be, how they want to be perceived, and how they are treated. Accomplishing such a lofty goal requires the invention of several different presentations of self. According to Jaclyn Suzuki, former creative director at Ziba Design, more than 75 percent of teens today feel comfortable having multiple online personas. For this generation, sharing different parts of their evolution with different peer groups isn't just accepted; it's required.

That's likely why Pivotals are sometimes referred to as the "slash" generation. Meaning, they can be a volleyball player/actress/fashionista/activist, switching out those descriptors as they see fit. After all, it only takes a simple swipe and upload to Instagram to change that outward identity combination.

"All someone has to do is look at my feed and within seconds they will know that I love to compete at CrossFit and snowboarding, wear preppy brands, worship the Minnesota Vikings, like rap and country, love Elon Musk, and have an insane infatuation with Gen Z," said Jonah Stillman in his book *Gen Z @ Work*, coauthored with his father, David Stillman. "If I wake up one day and decide I don't like Elon Musk, I simply hit 'delete.'"

Per a recent article in *Family Circle*, "Teens are beginning to discuss and approach their online reputations much like companies. They worry about their brand being consistent across profiles and posts. They test posts for 'virality,' trying to optimize likes, comments and shares with subsequent posts."[9]

Pivotals' brand value, recognition, and influence all depend on the amount of people engaging with and sharing their posts. Views, comments, likes, and retweets are all concrete measures of brand growth and success.

Of course, being adept brand managers, Pivotals know all this. They know when and where to post to get the most engagement. In a study conducted by creative agency Heat on behalf of its client, Teva, marketers found that most teens schedule posts for midday and evening in order to maximize engagement. In fact, almost 50 percent of teens post in the evening, and conduct 75 percent of social media activity on Fridays and Saturdays. They are calculated, strategic, and, honestly, rather impressive. Analytics are in their DNA, it's how they listen to the world around them. And brands failing to recognize trends in engagement aren't paying attention.

With so much data at their fingertips, Pivotal preferences should be blatantly obvious. "Should" being the key word there. Brands should recognize and respond to how Pivotals choose to present themselves on social media, how they outwardly express their gender identification (or lack thereof), and how they view the world. Pivotals are forcing brands to rethink what it means to define one's sense of self and what that means for brand interaction and purchase behavior.

Brands like CoverGirl are paying attention.

CoverGirl took a bold step forward in 2016 by choosing 17-year-old makeup artist and YouTube star James Charles as its first male brand representative, that is, "CoverBoy." Charles's social media stardom (based on his popular, over-the-top makeup tutorials) caught the attention of CoverGirl, who soon recruited him to be the face of the brand's new mascara, So Lashy. The mascara was created for every type of person and all types of lashes, a message of "lash equality" that James Charles clearly exemplifies. Since announcing his collaboration with CoverGirl, Charles has surpassed two million Instagram followers. Pivotals praised CoverGirl for embracing diversity and pushing boundaries.

Curation Overload

Social media is used to portray the fakest version of ourselves
that will fit society standards for what will make a cool, fun, unique
person. Social media creates a lens through which you view yourself
based on the opinions of other people.

—CONNOR BLAKLEY

Consider the story of Essena O'Neill. On the outside, O'Neill had it all: Instagram celebrity status, a modeling contract, and brands throwing money at her to promote products. However, in 2015, the then 18-year-old social media star suddenly deleted her accounts and publicly warned others of just how superficial Internet fame could be.

Before taking down her Instagram posts, she edited the captions to past posts to reveal what was truly happening behind the scenes. Many were posed and sponsored, one of which took more than 100 attempts on an empty stomach for O'Neill to look appealing in a bikini.

"I've spent the majority of my teenage life being addicted to social media, social approval, social status and my physical appearance," lamented O'Neill in an explanation post. "I was sick and I needed serious help."

O'Neill has since renamed her Instagram "Social Media Is Not Real Life" to enforce the idea that our society's obsession with constant image curation is neither healthy nor realistic. "Everything I did was for likes and for followers," she admitted. "I had never been more miserable."

The constant curation and perfect image took a serious toll on O'Neill. It went from making friends and looking her best to creating the appearance of perfection. The pressure was insane; her audience demanded images of beautiful and exotic landscapes interrupted only by her tan, trim, and tantalizing figure. Her true identity took a back seat as she created the perfect and most desirable identity. Presenting her "best self" was eclipsed by her "most desirable self."

O'Neill was able to regain control of her image, but, for many, the pressure to curate their lives crosses into dangerous territory. In fact, the rise of social media and technology has overlapped with a decline in mental health, per *Scientific American*. In 2014, psychologist Jean M. Twenge of San Diego State University studied data from nearly seven million teenagers and adults nationwide and found that teens now are twice as likely as teens in the 1980s to seek mental health treatment.[10] While many factors contribute to this trend, it's not unreasonable to believe that social media and the curation it requires is hurting the psyche of teens. Balancing self-expression with amassing followers can be a disastrous combination. This isn't to say social media is bad; in many cases, it can be a useful tool in connecting with others. But it is a ground where brands should tread lightly.

LISTEN TO BE HEARD

To reach Pivotals on such shaky ground means recognizing and understanding the extreme pressure they experience. Marketers, we must approach Pivotals as unique individuals and see them as engineers working to piece together their personal brands in a time when image is everything. A one-size-fits-all approach won't work.

We can't continue to create "voices" we *think* will appeal to them—telling them what we *think* they want to hear. We need to start sharing our *real* voice, having *real* conversations, and making *real* connections with them. Stop selling and start supporting. Prove we understand and see them as people. Make them feel heard and appreciated.

Sound impossible? It's not. In fact, it's quite simple. It starts with listening. Spend some time on Twitter and Instagram. What are teens talking about on social media? What are the hot topics or issues of the day, and how can your brand authentically contribute to those conversations?

From there, it's all about being down-to-earth and unfiltered in communications and messaging—aka humanizing the brand—something most companies aren't yet comfortable doing and understandably so. The traditional forms of marketing were to impress and allure. Today, with so many messages promising perfection, Pivotals are hungry for authentic communication. They have been marketed to their entire lives and can smell a promotional ploy or phony message from a mile away.

Emma Ryan, a Gen Zer and former intern at Wilde Agency, recommends something even more radical than just listening and humanizing. She suggests coming right out and telling Pivotals who you are, what you sell, and why they should buy it. In other words, zero tricks or gimmicks.

"Earn our respect and trust by being blunt and to the point," she explained in her blog post, "A Guide for Marketing to Generation Z: Be Blunt, Be Engaging + Be Trustworthy." "Tell us exactly what you're marketing and how much it costs. State that we should buy it because it rocks, it will improve our lives in some way, and you want our business, point blank."[11]

A healthy dose of honesty and originality takes a brand a long way in the eyes of Pivotals. Don't force-feed them what you think they want to hear.

"In an environment characterized by dramatically increasing levels of information and a limited ability to consume it, we have to do things differently—much differently—to stand out," said Mark Schaefer, author, speaker, and director of Schaefer Marketing Solutions, on his blog. "Over time, the most human companies will win."[12]

How "Brand You" Can Support "Brand Me"

In the not so distant past, young people happily sported flashy labels. The Ralph Lauren polo player, the Calvin Klein initial logo on jeans, and shirts that proudly read "Abercrombie and Fitch" were aspirational symbols for Millennials. However, the free advertising train has come to a screeching halt.

Major apparel companies, who traditionally succeed with heavily branded garments, are seeing sales decline at a staggering rate. According to Abercrombie's 2016 Annual Investor Report, retail sales have been on the decline for the past three years.[13]

Pivotals couldn't care less about your logo. In fact, they are repulsed by the idea of paying their hard earned money to wear your logo. They're all public figures after all. If anything, you should be paying *them*.

Wearing words "Hollister and Co." across the chest of a T-shirt doesn't have the same impact it once did. The lack of subtlety is off-putting. Instead, Pivotals are attracted to brands that can help them curate and manage Brand Me. No matter what you sell or promote, your priority should be helping, empowering, and even collaborating with Pivotals. Take your logo out of the spotlight, and let their image shine.

Pivotals don't run from a challenge. Even when confronted with plummeting self-image, Essena O'Neill took control and dove head-first into solving the problem. Pivotals aren't afraid to get their hands dirty or put in the hard work necessary to achieve success.

In this way, Pivotals want to be their own heroes—not the innocent bystanders to big brands. Instead of promising to be the end-all-be-all solution, successful brands will support Pivotals in achieving their goals, whether big or small.

How do you accomplish this? Let's explore four approaches.

Reflect Their Values

To protect their brand image, Pivotals align only with brands reflective of worthy values. Any association with a harmful, ignorant, exploitative, or hateful situation is quickly met with vocal disapproval. As for the opposite? Integrity and compassion are consistently met with vocal *praise*.

CASE STUDY

Who: American Eagle

What: Even when so many other teen brands have failed, American Eagle (AE) continues to find success. It consciously decided to embrace individuality and forego the commercialism of gendered stereotypes and logos stitched across products long before its competitors, choosing to feature a cast of diverse young adult models from a variety of ethnic backgrounds. In addition to their cultural differences, these models also vary in size and shape, wearing the brand apparel in their own distinct way.

How: Most recently this can be seen in the brand's We All Can, Can You? campaign, which promotes individualism, diversity, and teens' interest in being self-expressive. Visuals of the campaign feature statements such as "I can love anyone," "I can be heard," "I can create my future," and "I can fear nothing." Additionally, the campaign features some of the most popular influencers of Gen Z today, including Hailee Steinfeld, Valentina Cytrynowicz, and Xiao Wen Ju.

"[Gen Zers] are not judgmental, they don't put people in boxes, and they don't seem to care as much about what you do, who you love, or what you look like," said AE CMO Kyle Andrew in an interview with *Fast Company*. "Generation Z seems to really care about engaging with brands that have values that align with their own."

Andrews' advice for brands? "You can't just make stuff: You have to stand for something."

Fast-fashion brand H&M is another example of a brand that reflects Pivotals' values.

CASE STUDY

Who: H&M

What: Popular among Millennials for its affordable yet stylish apparel, H&M has also found a way to resonate with Gen Z through its decision to celebrate the independence and free will of women in its She's a Lady campaign.

How: Redefining the traditional standards of "ladylike," the ads feature a cast of different sizes, shapes, ethnicities, and cultural backgrounds who have varying personal interests and takes on style. Throughout, a remake by Lion Babe of Tom Jones's hit song of the same name plays in the background, one that takes on a whole new meaning for feminism than the original.

An H&M spokesperson explained, "The latest campaign celebrates diversity as well as inspirational women from various backgrounds, encouraging women around the world to embrace their personal style and take pride in who they truly are and what they stand for."

Impact: Because of this stance, the brand has received praise online and more than 57 million hits on YouTube.

But it isn't just one campaign that has exhibited H&M's strong feelings on social equality. In 2016, the brand made waves for featuring Mariah Idrissi, a Muslim of Pakistani and Moroccan heritage, in her hijab and a pair of the brand's sunglasses. The video she was featured in, "Close the Loop," also

featured other cast members of various nationalities, gen-
ders, and sizes.

Idrissi had nothing but positive thoughts to share on the
effort, sharing with CNN in an interview: "They actually really knew exactly how I should be dressed. They understood it
had to be very loose fitting, not figure hugging, not anything
revealing. They gave a range of different outfits . . . all of them
were respectable."[14]

Build Trust Through Transparency

While the road to authenticity and trust is steep, the payoff is a mul-
tiplier. Brands must not only be transparent in their story; they must
allow consumers to ask the difficult questions and be prepared to respond honestly. Additionally, brands must be transparent in all actions
and decisions, ranging from sourcing to distribution to staffing.

Pivotals will never love your brand without trust, which must be
earned. The only way to earn that trust is through consistency over
time. Brands that are transparent in their beliefs and actions while
providing quality products that support Pivotals' quest for uniqueness
and in-the-know status on the latest and greatest products are best
positioned for success with this generation.

CASE STUDY

Who: Nike

What: While Nike is not a brand segmented to one generation
of consumers, it has built up trust with Pivotals due to its
dedication to a purpose that is much deeper than just selling
gear. In fact, Nike built its brand on this purpose: Everyone is
an athlete. Thus, it established an authority that extends be-

yond the production of shoes and fitness apparel and into the lives of those who interact with the brand. On a deeply human level, Nike connects with its consumers and supports them in identifying as an athlete, regardless of talent or experience.

How: The brand's Unlimited campaign that debuted in 2016 championed the stories of athletes including Chris Mosier, the first transgender athlete on a U.S. National Team; Kyle Maynard, the first quadruple amputee to climb Mount Kilimanjaro; and Sister Madonna Buder, an 86-year-old Catholic nun and triathlete. The ads focused on each athlete's unique strengths and attributes, using slogans to highlight them: Unlimited Will, Unlimited Courage, Unlimited Fight, Unlimited Pursuit, and so on.

Impact: In addition to promoting diversity in its advertising and marketing, Nike has also done so through its business model. In an act of transparency, the brand released data on its internal structure last year, allowing the world to see that the majority of its employees are members of minorities and that women make up 48 percent of its entire global workforce.[15] This solidified Nike as a brand that both talks the talk and walks the walk.

Engage Them

Brand engagement is pivotal in this day and age, and brands cannot survive without it: It's comparable to the absolute necessity of having a website two decades ago.

—VICTOR DE VITA, "CREATING BRAND DESIRE: FINDING THE GENERATION Z 'SWEET SPOT'"[16]

The best way to reach Pivotals is to directly engage with them and make them part of your brand story. They've got amazing ideas, so let them help design your products and/or promote your brand. Feature them in your marketing efforts as well. User-generated content is astoundingly effective, as 92 percent of people trust another person over branded content, even if they don't know the person.[17] If you bring Pivotals into your inner circle and treat them like trusted friends, that's exactly what they'll become.

CASE STUDY

Who: Chubbies

What: The men's shorts start-up resonates with Pivotals because of its relatable content and strong brand message. Its four founders started the retro-inspired brand to stand out from more serious men's fashion brands, and they champion a message of inclusivity, self-expression, and fun.

The reason it's so successful? "We're really built around our customer as our friend," says Tom Montgomery, one of the founders. He credits Chubbies' customers for generating content and word-of-mouth endorsements, claiming that "it really is a community building this business."

How: One reason Pivotals relate to Chubbies is because it engages actual customers as models, beer bellies and dad bods included. This not only gets customers involved in the business, but it preserves authenticity. Montgomery considers Chubbies' relationship with its consumers reciprocal. "The second we become transactional is the moment we take a misstep," he states. "We need to be providing value just like they provide value to us in the business."

Impact: This marketing strategy has earned the brand some incredible results. Across all social media channels, Chubbies garnered 350 million video views in 2016 alone, as well as one of the most viewed online advertisements of the summer Olympics. The video, featuring actual male customers of all shapes and sizes, presents a comedic synchronized swimming routine. Part of the brilliance of Chubbies' social strategy is its team's constantly creating and adjusting content based on customer feedback.

Montgomery advises treating your brand like a person to avoid content stagnation. "People are constantly trying to keep the conversation fresh and genuine, and that's the same interaction with a brand."

Inspire Them (and Let Them Inspire You)

Whether it's shocking, amusing, sad, or even off-putting, marketers should focus on eliciting an *emotional* response, as the customer is two to three times more likely to purchase a product based on the emotional response to an advertisement rather than the content of the ad.[18]

CASE STUDY

Who: Russell Athletic

What: In 2015, Russell Athletic (a Barkley client) chose to relaunch its 100-year-old brand as the "Expert and Defender of Team." So instead of partnering with the pros and individual egos like most other brands of the sports apparel industry, Russell Athletic partnered with real high school teams. And while sports marketing traditionally celebrates the winners, Russell Athletic focused on the untold stories of sports. Partnering with six of the 101 schools that lost the state championship by a touchdown or less the previous year—Russell Athletic turned the loss that haunted these teams into their ultimate motivation.

How: Using the tagline #SettleYourScore, Russell launched a campaign with a series of short videos showcasing how high school football coaches help players build character and resilience through the lessons learned in defeat.

As motivation for the team to stare down their demons, Russell Athletic blanketed communities in the 2016 preseason with billboards, banners, fan signage, and T-shirts emblazoned with each team's mantra for every window, player, parent, and local fan to remind them that what haunts them *fuels* them in the new season. In addition, Russell partnered with legendary *Friday Night Lights* photographer Robert Clark. He documented one team's preparation for a comeback in his iconic, raw, and emotion-evoking style through film and photography. Russell Athletic also partnered with the school's student photographers to help tell the story through their own eyes while partnering with SB Nation and Vox Media to create four additional documentary films.

"This is a very compelling and unique way to tell untold stories," explains Matt Murphy, Russell Athletic senior vice president of marketing. "It put the Russell Athletic brand at the center of our rich heritage—born on the playing fields of America."

Impact: The emotional authenticity and relatability of the underdog story are why the marketing campaign has received such positive feedback, according to Berk Wasserman, Barkley VP and creative director. "It speaks to sports fans and to a much larger audience, because it's a story we can all relate to." By partnering with media companies, high school teams, and a renowned photographer, the campaign taught teams, and in turn teens, that even the most devastating loss can become the ultimate motivation.

WHAT IT ALL MEANS

From customers to fans, from fans to partners, Pivotals are active participants in your brand story. They aren't just your customers; Pivotals are your most trusted advisors. With years of experience under their belts, they are your best resource in building a brand worth following. They get it, and they want you to get it too.

So, if you haven't already, it's time to invite Pivotals to the party. Maybe even ask them to show up early and help decorate. While it can be a bit scary to invite customers in before the proverbial streamers are up, it's essential to establishing trust. If Pivotals are expressing themselves, you should be too. They want authenticity, so walk alongside them as they experiment and evolve.

Curating a brand is hard. Pivotals know that more than most, so stop hiding. Encourage, support, and see them as they want to be seen. Help them establish a new "slash" in their Instagram bio and laugh at their jokes. Brand Me is all about being understood and accepted, so ditch the buyer personas and customer voice calculations. Pivotals are excited to talk to you. They're excited to share their perfectly manicured Instagram profile with someone who understands. They've invested years into their brand and expect the same from you.

KEY TAKEAWAYS

- **Pivotals value being seen as unique,** but not so unique they don't fit in. They seek validation, as well as acceptance, from their peers.

- **Pivotals obsess more about their appearance than generations past.** Because their curated identities are so public, teens are hyperconscious of the way they present themselves.

- **Pivotals view their identity as a curated composition built over time.** That composition starts at a young age and is constantly evolving.

- **No matter what brands sell or promote, the priority should be helping, empowering, and even collaborating with Pivotals.** Instead of promising to be the end-all-be-all solution, successful brands will support Pivotals in achieving their goals.

- **Pivotals align themselves with brands that reflect their values.** Any association with a harmful or ignorant situation is met with vocal disapproval, while integrity and compassion are met with praise.

NEW KIDS ON THE
SHOPPING BLOCK

Today's empowered customers no longer purchase products; they buy experiences. They engage with brands that deliver what they need, when they need it, regardless of the delivery mechanism or channel.

**—"THE RISE OF THE EMPOWERED CUSTOMER,"
FORRESTER RESEARCH, 2016**

On track to make up 40 percent of consumers by 2020, the future of retail is without a doubt in Pivotals' hands. Yet most retailers are nowhere near ready for the most demanding and empowered shoppers the world has ever known.

Forrester defines empowered customers as those who are open to new experiences, who show increasingly advanced device behaviors and digital expectations, who can easily seek, evaluate, and share information, and who are willing to take ownership of their decisions to ensure the best possible experience.[1]

Sounds like a dictionary definition of Pivotals, doesn't it? These empowered young customers don't see a difference between their physical and digital worlds—they simply assume everything will blend together seamlessly. Their expectations of speed and personalization are challenging brands and shattering traditional business models. And their lust for researching products and seeking input from peers before making a purchase is changing the shopper journey forever.

What's more, they've grown up with the "Big A"—Amazon, the e-commerce powerhouse that has single-handedly reinvented the shopping experience. Amazon is doing everything right: obsessively focusing on customer wants and needs, innovating at every turn, and making the shopping experience both enjoyable and easy. In turn, this is what Pivotals have come to expect from every shopping experience, not just on Amazon. We call it the "Amazon effect."

That's a high bar and one that presents a daunting challenge for most traditional retailers and brands. What will it take to compete with Amazon for the hearts, minds, and wallets of Pivotal consumers?

Before we explore a few ideas, let's first take a peek inside their piggy banks.

MONEY MATTERS

Pivotals might be young, and they might use acronyms and communicate in memes, but they have serious power. And they're carrying it around in their pockets.

The Pivotal generation has big-time pocket cash. They've amassed $44 billion of their own money from allowances and jobs. When you factor in their incredible influence over family spending decisions, that number skyrockets.

However, all that money isn't burning holes in their pockets. Pivotals are savings minded; they're frugal, savvy consumers who expect more for their money than the generations before them. Like Millennials, they value experiences over things and aren't interested in accumulating debt. In fact, according to Experian, Pivotals have three times less debt than Boomers.[2]

Sure, they're at a different life stage and have had less time to pile up debt, but with many of them entering college—with student loans and credit cards available at every turn—they have had ample opportunity to dig themselves a debt sinkhole. But instead of indulging during their youth, Pivotals have chosen a more financially stable future.

According to Student Loan Hero, the Pivotal generation is more money-smart than previous generations, with:

1. Fewer credit cards and less debt than previous generations
2. Less debt from the get-go
3. Greater expectations for their money
4. A preference for saving their money
5. A focus on striving for career and financial stability[3]

While Pivotal parents couldn't be happier about this, retailers are feeling the pressure. Predicting sales for this demographic is difficult and sometimes discouraging. Take heart, however. It's not all doom and gloom. Pivotals *will* spend money when they see the value in a product or experience. In fact, they'll spend more than 50 percent of what they earn monthly, per the "Uniquely Generation Z" study.[4]

The question is, how do we, as marketers, convince them to spend that money on our brand, product, or service?

THE PIVOTAL SHOPPING JOURNEY

Oh, how marketers long for the good ol' days of the traditional shopper journey. You know, when we could predictably map consumer behavior, step by step, through the phases of the classic sales and marketing funnel: awareness, opinion, consideration, preference, and purchase. If we did our jobs right, shoppers would start at the top of the funnel—awareness—and move through the linear steps as we, along with our sales team, expertly guided them toward purchase and ultimately brand loyalty. (See Figure 6-1.)

But today, alas, the old rules no longer apply. With so much information, touchpoints with consumers—especially uber-informed, discerning yet attention-challenged Pivotal consumers—are anything *but* linear. Marketing and sales teams have to work together to reach and satisfy consumers along the winding path of the *customer's* choosing.

Figure 6-1 The traditional shopping journey.

For Pivotals, the path doesn't start with traditional mass advertising; it starts with social media and their friend networks, with the mobile phone as the conduit. And they almost always do their research first, with only 6 percent of that research done in stores![5]

As discussed in Chapter 4, their peers wield the most influence when it comes to buying decisions. A 2017 global consumer shopping survey by Accenture shows 44 percent of Gen Z cite social media as a popular source of product inspiration.

Retail and brand consultancy Fitch says there is also a big gap between seeing and buying for the Gen Z consumer that doesn't exist with older shoppers. Michelle Fenstermaker, strategy director at Fitch, calls this the "aspirational browsing" period: It's all about "the hunt, creating a scrapbook, and broadcasting their potential purchases and seeking input from their social circles."[6] (See Figure 6-2.)

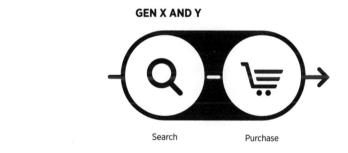

GEN X AND Y

Search   Purchase

GEN Z

Aspirational browse
All about the hunt
Creating a scrapbook
Broadcasting potential purchases

Search   Purchase

Figure 6-2 Aspirational browsing.[7]

This makes perfect sense. More than half of respondents to a 2017 survey from the HRC Retail Advisory showed Gen Zers use social media to gather opinions while shopping, and more than 40 percent make purchase decisions based on that peer feedback.

In addition to the aspirational browsing period, we're also intrigued by Fitch's concept of a five-stage purchase path for Gen Z consumers, which starts with finding out about products through a variety of touch-points, including peer suggestion, websites, social media influencers, unplanned store visits, and certain types of advertising. (See Figure 6-3.)

Once inspired, they go online to browse, most often using Google. Engaging with Pivotals where they search is an absolute *must*. Most advertising methods interrupt the user's life and take a gamble on whether or not the user is primed to buy. However, search engine optimization (SEO) and pay-per-click ads put your message in front of consumers the very minute they are looking for your product. It's not a new or sexy marketing tactic, but it is wildly effective. However, keep in mind that Pivotals are conditioned to immediately skip down to the fourth link since the first three links are typically paid advertise-ments. Pivotals trust organic search results much more than paid ads, so a strong SEO strategy is crucial.

Regardless of what search marketing method your brand uses, once Google deems you worthy and Pivotals click on your site, you are now

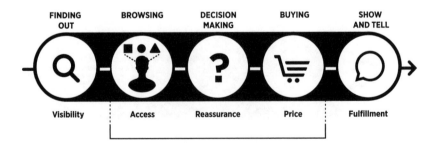

Figure 6-3 Five-stage purchase path.[8]

responsible for how long they stay. While most generations browse only the first page and then "bounce" away, Pivotals are 51 percent less likely to leave before exploring further, according to a recent ebook by ContentSquare, *Generation Z: The Coming of (Shopping) Age.*

Given their willingness to explore and preference for abbreviated content, Pivotals are giving marketers ample opportunity to tell their story.

Yet even if they love the story you have to tell, never expect a Pivotal to buy on the first visit. These frugal shoppers enjoy the thrill of the hunt and won't hand over their dollars until they've tracked down the best deal. (See Figure 6-3.)

This leads the Pivotals to begin the third stage: decision making. Regardless of how compelling your value offering may be, Pivotals will leave to comparison shop and crowdsource opinions. To bypass this conversion-killing phase, consider setting up an online review platform. Pivotals *read* them (as well as *write* them). They'll also seek out reviews on third-party blogs and websites, but if you make it easier for them to find and read reviews on *your* site first, that might satisfy their need for validation.

While on the hunt for consumer validation, Pivotals will also aggressively price shop. So, while a product testimonial will win over their heart, price comparisons are the only way to win over their mind. Many Pivotals check for discounts or similar products on Amazon, eBay, or other bargain sites. Or, like Angie's 13-year-old daughter, some will even check with friends to see whether they have the same or similar product at home and whether they might be interested in trading or selling it. Talk about a serious hunt!

Finally, perhaps the most interesting part of Fitch's five-stage purchase path is a relatively new phenomenon that Pivotals learned from Millennials, called the "show-and-tell" phase. This is when Gen Z shoppers immediately connect with their peers, sharing pictures or videos of their purchases with their social networks once they get home (sometimes referred to as "hauls"). But here's the kicker: If they don't get the

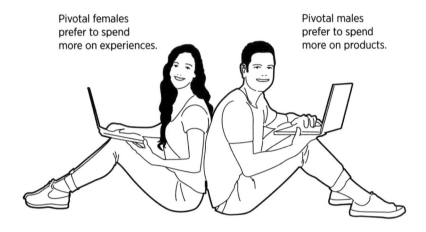

Pivotal females prefer to spend more on experiences.

Pivotal males prefer to spend more on products.

Figure 6-4 Shopping preferences by gender.

response they want or expect, Gen Z won't hesitate to return the item(s).

No surprise, young men and women have different spending preferences. Per a national study by the Center for Generational Kinetics, "The State of Gen Z 2017: Meet the Throwback Generation," Pivotal guys prefer to spend more on products (like clothes, electronics, and technology), while Pivotal girls want to spend more on experiences (like eating out with friends, going to the movies, or attending concerts). (See Figure 6-4.)

Long Live the Mall

It's a pleasurable experience. It's the joy of the hunt that they're looking for.

—MARK MATHEWS, "GENERATION Z: A PRIMER ON THEIR SHOPPING AND FASHION HABITS"[9]

But where are they completing their purchases? After everything we've covered in this book so far, one might assume Pivotals shop only on their phones. Surprise! Pivotals still love to hit the mall.

What the Internet tries to mimic, the mall still owns. Touching, feeling, and trying on clothes will always be superior to online sizing charts. No social media platform in the world can compete with a best friend, and no drone on the planet can deliver a new pair of shoes as fast as a teen can carry them out of the store. (See Figure 6-5.)

Yes, there are still lines to deal with and inventory headaches, but seeing merchandise firsthand is an experience all its own. Pivotals recognize that. According to a July 2016 study from Retail Perceptions, teens prefer to buy food, health and beauty products, shoes, and clothes in person. This can mainly be attributed to the try-before-you-buy benefit, but don't overlook the perks of helpful sales associates. Pivotals will not part with their cash unless they fully understand what they're buying and how it's going to help them. Without a professional to lead the way, health and beauty can be confusing and overwhelming, giving physical stores an upper hand. Buying a $30 facewash is a lot less intimidating when you have an expert showing you how it works.

The instant gratification, helpful service, and changing rooms are the big reasons why 72 percent of teens still go to the mall at least

PROS
- Seeing merchandise firsthand
- Browsing in stores
- Getting products immediately
- In-person advice from store associates
- Personalized experience

CONS
- Lines
- Lack of inventory; wrong sizes

Figure 6-5 Pros and cons of shopping in the store.[10]

once a month, according to a recent HRC Retail Advisory survey. However, what's interesting about those mall visits is the length of time spent shopping. Yes, most trips last about one hour. But that one hour is spread among up to five stores, nearly eliminating the opportunity for window shopping.[11] Pivotals aren't hanging out with their friends, meandering from store to store; they have a mission in mind. Stores that previously relied on foot traffic and the casual browser will suffer as teens zero in on their goals.

In 2017, Macy's, J.C. Penney, The Limited, and even long-time teen favorite Wet Seal all suffered massive store closures. Many experts attribute the cause to an imbalance of supply and demand; there are simply too many stores for America to patronize. Even Richard Hayne, the CEO of Urban Outfitters (still quite popular with teens), says the retail market is oversaturated.

"Our industry, not unlike the housing industry, saw too much square footage capacity added in the 1990s and early 2000s. Thousands of new doors opened and rents soared. This created a bubble, and like housing, that bubble has now burst," Hayne said.

The carnage of the retail bubble is visible in almost every city. Large buildings and in some cases entire malls are left vacant. Pivotals are indifferent to food courts and summer sales; a meaningful experience is what draws them in.

CASE STUDY

Who: Urban Outfitters

What: The fashion brand has been making strides in experimental retail by turning their brick-and-mortar stores into more than just a place to buy clothes, that is, "retail-tainment"—a combination of retail and entertainment, according to Joanna Ewing, Urban Outfitters' chief executive global creative director.[12]

How: Urban Outfitters' Lifestyle Center in New York's Herald Square comprises a hair salon, coffee shop, new technology, and more in its 57,000-square-foot location. Store locations around the country regularly host events, parties, and concerts to revolutionize the shopping experience.

"That's what we're dead-set on creating, these experiences, because our customer is in the most exciting time of their lives," said Ewing of the brand's move toward cultivating real-life connections and moments.

Impact: In the midst of the modern-day struggle to keep customers shopping in-store rather than online, Urban Outfitters engages the Pivotal consumer by offering more than the average retailer in novel, ever-evolving ways. Indeed, brands targeting the elusive Gen Z must be constantly changing to retain the generation's short attention span.

"By creating a community feeling through extra additions like a library or cafe, not only are we promoting our lifestyle, but we are also creating a new retail environment for customers to discover and enjoy," said Stephen Briars, former Urban Outfitters creative director.[13]

IN-STORE SHOPPING: ALL ABOUT THE EXPERIENCE

Succeeding as a brick-and-mortar store today is less about setting up the perfect display and more about melding the technology consumers love with the items you sell. Teens expect the ability to locate products via their mobile devices or download special offers from the store's app, as well as the choice to pay via mobile or self-checkout.

Subtler in-store experiences can also play a major role, such as the integration of upbeat music and friendly, helpful sales people—anything that makes the customer experience more personal, engaging, and fun. And, of course, the lowest hanging fruit of all: free Wi-Fi.

Plus, don't forget the basics! Ensure that store associates are there to assist, not push. Answer questions, not "sell." And, above all, treat Pivotals with respect and appreciation. Any hint of being talked down to or disregarded will send them straight into the arms of your competitor. In essence, create an experience worth Snapping about.

Neiman Marcus saw the writing on the wall and found a creative way to bring tech into the changing rooms. The luxury department store installed 3D Augmented Reality Mirrors, referred to as "Magic Mirrors," in 34 locations to supplement their customer service and

Figure 6-6 Rendering of a "Magic Mirror."

allow consumers to try on various products and accessories "magically." (See Figure 6-6.)

By bringing digital innovation into the physical space, brands optimize the customer experience and create more confident and informed customers.

CASE STUDY

Who: Apple

What: For an example of a brand that has seamlessly integrated the digital and in-store experiences, just look at Apple.

How: Inside the store, Apple merges personable customer service with a digital experience. Associates equipped with iPads assist customers, who can try out any device before purchasing. Some people visit the Apple store without any intent of purchasing but just to have a chance to play with the newest technology! Even payment is done digitally, without a cash register in sight. Online, consumers can research merchandise and even order it to their home or their local Apple store. Merchandise can be ordered during in-store visits as well. The all-encompassing Apple ID allows customers to use all Apple programs and services, log into the App Store from any device, check in at the physical store, participate in online discussions or support, and access iCloud. Even within their product lineup, there exists a cohesion in which it makes sense for a consumer to buy more Apple products so as to get full functionality from other Apple products.

> **Impact:** Apple has built a reputation for staying far ahead of its competitors in every aspect of the business. Its products are easy to use, and its customer service is easy to access, whether online, in person, or on another platform completely.
>
> As Brent Franson, CEO of Euclid Analytics, boasts, "You've got the product playground that is the physical experience, supplemented by human beings that can answer questions—all done by the umbrella of a single 'Apple ID.'"[14]

Online Shopping: Convenient and Efficient

Generation Z expects technology to be intuitive, relevant and engaging—their last great experience is their new expectation.

—STEVE LAUGHLIN, "JOINT PRESS RELEASE: IBM AND NRF: DESPITE LIVING A DIGITAL LIFE, 98 PERCENT OF GENERATION Z STILL SHOP IN-STORE"[15]

Online shopping is a solution to the two main Pivotal complaints about shopping in stores: lines and inventory issues. While brick-and-mortar stores are still a favorite with Pivotals, they *are* shopping online and will do so in greater numbers as technology continues to make shopping easier and faster. After all, they're digital natives raised in a post-Amazon world. They're hardwired for "clicks over bricks."

This isn't unique to Pivotals. Shoppers of all ages have figured this out, especially on crazy shopping holidays like Black Friday. It's much easier to shop from the comfort of your home, avoiding lines and rowdy crowds, checking online inventory, searching for discounts, then having your purchases delivered right to your door a few days later.

However, for Pivotals, that shopping experience is at its best when it works as expected, which is flawlessly. In the "Uniquely Generation

Z" study, almost half of Gen Zers surveyed said that, while shopping, the most important factor is the ability to find things quickly, and more than 60 percent refuse to use apps or websites that are hard to navigate or slow to load.[16]

On the other hand, if your site works perfectly, the rewards are real. ContentSquare reports that Pivotals convert about twice as much as the rest of the population.[17] So keep that old saying in mind, "You only get one chance to make a first impression." Make sure their first online shopping experience with you makes a positive impression. Make it easy for them to get in, find what they want, place their order, and get out. If they can't do that, your competitor is just a click away.

"User experience is the new salesperson and customer support," said Jonathan Cherki, founder and CEO of ContentSquare. "Gone are the days of a one-size-fits-all user experience. In the future, user experience will be the new brand." Everything in a digital storefront—from color scheme to image selection to check-out word choice—should work together to tell a brand's story.

Need for Speed

While we're talking about user experience, let's dive right into a huge component of establishing a positive vibe: speed.

Pivotals want everything to be *fast*. It's one of the reasons they still shop in-store—instant gratification. They won't think twice about canceling an online order if the delivery window is either ambiguous or will take longer than a few days.

If they have the option of getting something same-day, they're also more than happy to pay a premium for that luxury. Per a recent Temando survey, 61 percent of respondents would choose the option of same-day delivery even if it meant paying a surcharge. Fifty-eight percent said they'd pay even more than for *one-hour* deliveries.[18] One hour! Again, patience is not a virtue of the Pivotal generation.

Conversely, as frugal, value-oriented shoppers, they're sensitive to shipping costs and often prioritize affordability over convenience. According to the same Temando report, more than half of Pivotal shoppers abandon their online shopping carts if shipping costs aren't ideal, even if they've completed every other portion of the purchase process.

Retailers should offer a variety of online shipping options, then follow through on those delivery promises. Or use free shipping as a marketing tactic to drive sales, like offering free shipping if they meet a spend threshold. Pivotals want speedy shipping, *and* they expect their favorite brands to deliver. Zing!

Social Buying

In the perfect marriage of form and function, social buying is the biggest win for both consumers and marketers. In the Dark Ages before social buying, if you saw a shirt you liked on a passing stranger, you were resigned to endless Google searches for "cool shirt with birds on it."

Today, when a Pivotal watches a YouTube video and sees his or her favorite influencer wearing a cool shirt, they simply click "Buy now." That's it. Just one click.

Facebook integrates seamlessly with e-commerce, Polyvore lets users create dream outfits using real products, and Pinterest gives brands the power to pin their products, their prices, and even their *inventory.* Social buying apps like Venmo turn sharing the check into a social life hack. The key with social buying is to layer ease of purchase with a social experience. Plugging social media into your website or adding a "Buy now" button to your Instagram is not social buying: Creating an environment where discovery naturally flows to purchase is.

WHAT IT ALL MEANS

Gen Zers are changing the shopping game. They're still going to malls and shopping in physical stores, but they're doing it their own way. Getting the youngest yet most sophisticated consumers to open their (virtual) wallets requires dedication to both your online *and* your offline shopping experiences and ensuring they work together seamlessly. Pivotals demand efficiency, speed, and a wide range of options, coupled with helpful service. Whether they are in-store or online, their expectations remain the same.

Brands with the means to innovate on a grand scale, through Magic Mirrors and the like, win with Pivotals, but improving the shopping experience is accessible to brands of all sizes. The goal isn't to impress but to engage. Think through the shopping experience, weigh the strengths and weaknesses of your online and offline stores, and develop a strategy that makes the process faster, easier, and more enjoyable. We mentioned Wi-Fi, apps, social buttons, and mobile-optimized websites, but those are simply a jumping-off point. What does your brand do well? How are Pivotals making purchase decisions? Can they find you online? How can you satisfy their needs early and often?

Pivotals haven't lost interest in brick-and-mortar stores; they just see those buildings as a single element of a much bigger shopping experience. They aren't ignoring the sales funnel or fighting tradition; Pivotals just expect value and excellence from every interaction. So should you.

■　　■　　■

KEY TAKEAWAYS

- **Pivotals participate in a so-called aspirational browsing period before actually making a purchase.** It's all about searching for and broadcasting potential purchases on social media to seek input from their peers.

- **Teens prefer to buy food, health and beauty products, shoes, and clothes in person.** Pivotals will not part with their cash unless they fully understand what they're buying and how it's going to help them.

- **For Pivotals, the online shopping experience is better than in-store only when it works flawlessly.** Speed and convenience are necessities!

- **In the perfect marriage of form and function, social buying is the biggest win for both consumers and marketers.** The key with social buying is to create an environment where discovery naturally flows to purchase.

- **Pivotals expect value and excellence from every shopping interaction.** Make sure your brand delivers both.

HOT BRANDS AND COOL IDEAS

A brand for a company is like a reputation for a person. You earn
reputation by trying to do hard things well.

—JEFF BEZOS, "ONLINE EXTRA: JEFF BEZOS
ON WORD-OF-MOUTH POWER"[1]

Remember, it's all about Brand Me. Gen Z consumers expect to be
at the center of every brand's universe. They demand an experience
catered to their individual needs at any given moment. This means
that modern brands must offer opportunities for both personalization
and customization in a unique and meaningful way.

Brands are struggling to meet these demands. According to a
2017 study from American Express and Forrester, "Raising the Bar:
How Gen Z Expectations Are Reshaping Brand Experiences," Pivotals aren't satisfied with the speed, security, and experience of most
brands today. The same report urges brands to stay focused on the
customer to suit this "new world order of empowered and entitled
consumerism."[2]

Pivotals are looking for brands that offer something no one else
can. They value brands that lean into their unique strengths and offer
an uncommon solution to a common problem. Even then, if two
brands solving the same problem land around the same price point,

Pivotals look deeper for the winner. Just as with the Millennial generation before them, there is one key way brands can resonate with Pivotals: by offering *Proof of Purpose*.

STORYLIVING™

Great brands understand today's consumer requires proof. Brands are helping consumers co-create their own unique story. Proof of Purpose isn't a creative slogan or clever marketing campaign. Proof of Purpose consists of the visible steps a company takes to prove its values and beliefs. How is your brand committed to making the world a better place? Is your brand a force for good? How is your brand aligned with the core values and ideals of young consumers?

Pivotals aren't just buying *what* you do. They are buying into *why* you do it.

Brands like P&G and Unilever, for instance, effuse brand purpose. P&G is known for its Like a Girl campaign, which aims to empower women and girls. Yes, the brand sells feminine hygiene products, a rather "unsexy" product, but what it sold with its Like a Girl campaign was much more. P&G was showing its Proof of Purpose. It made clear its belief in girls and women and inspired thousands, maybe even millions to revisit their perception of women. P&G sees females as powerful creatures, both capable and strong, and it invited its consumers to see the same.

Similarly, Unilever let its true purpose shine through Unilever Foundry, a global crowdsourcing platform aimed at solving sustainability issues in sanitation, hygiene, and nutrition. It invites start-ups and innovative thinkers to work together as the brand grows, all with the community in mind.

"Purpose is about what you do and not what you say, and within the boardroom it has become a business transformation idea rather than a loose wrap-around at a brand level," said John Rudaizky, partner and global brand and external communications leader at Ernst and Young.[3]

In an age when consumers are more demanding yet less trusting, brands with the courage to stand for something will create emotional connections with consumers. As we've said throughout the book, personal connection is key with Pivotals—the gateway to trust.

"Young people prioritize one-to-one relationships and personal connections, and they don't switch off this mindset when they shop," says Cassandra Senior Editorial Director Melanie Shreffler to Marketing Dive. "They want to feel a personal connection with the brands they buy and support, and expect that brands, in turn, treat them as people, not just customers."[4]

Quite simply—yet not at all simple to do—brands that want to win with Pivotals must connect with them as unique individuals. It's about making and maintaining personal connections and providing superior value every step of the consumer journey. Yet brand effort can't stop there. There's still another and arguably more important bridge for brands to cross: *the bridge to brand loyalty.*

IS BRAND LOYALTY DEAD?

I don't think brand loyalty is dead; I think brand effort is dead.

—CONNOR BLAKLEY

Brand loyalty was strong with previous generations, where quality, price, and consistency won lifelong fidelity. Today, Pivotals pledge fealty only if Proof of Purpose is also at play.

While brand loyalty may be on the decline, it's not because Pivotals *can't* be loyal. It's because most brands haven't yet *earned* their loyalty.

Most marketers haven't even scratched the surface with Pivotals; how can we expect them to pledge allegiance to our brands?

Plus, they're young! Their inclination for brand loyalty may change over time, especially if we do our jobs correctly. But in the meantime the data isn't pretty.

Per 2017 research from Accenture:

- ▶ Sixteen percent of Gen Zers shop at a single store for clothing/ fashion (compared with 26 percent of millennials).
- ▶ Nineteen percent shop at a single store for health and beauty items (compared with 34 percent of millennials).
- ▶ Fewer than 38 percent shop at a single place for groceries (compared with 55 percent of Millennials).[5]

Another study from Retail Perceptions reviewed Pivotals' loyalty to their favorite brands:

- ▶ Eighty-one percent will switch from their favorite brand to a similar product at a higher quality.
- ▶ Seventy-nine percent indicate their preference is a quality product, not necessarily a name-brand item.
- ▶ Seventy-two percent will switch if they find a similar product for a lower price.[6]

If you went cross-eyed looking at all those numbers, the gist is this: Pivotals go where they get the most value.

Breaking into the Pivotals consideration set means overcoming two main obstacles:

Obstacle 1—Price and quality expectations: Striking a balance is tricky, but the principle is simple. Price must reflect quality. Charging high prices for low-quality products yields angry and very vocal customers. Charging low prices for a high-quality product triggers red flags and requires credibility through peer reviews.

Obstacle 2—Supporting their goals: Brands must help Pivotals cultivate their personal (and ever-evolving) identities, while simultaneously keeping the message relevant to their value proposition. This means creating products that are on-trend, make a statement, make their lives easier, showcase innovation, and/or help make the world a better place. A common strategy today is offering entertaining or informative content. If they go to you for information, they're likely to return for product recommendations.

Overcoming those obstacles, while difficult, yields a mutually beneficial relationship centered around trust. Yes, it's a lot of work, but it's absolutely worth it. Take a look at the following brands who fought the good fight and won over the Pivotal Generation. Well, for now.

10 BRANDS PIVOTALS LOVE

In one study conducted, we found Pivotals consider Nike, Apple, Target, and Netflix to be among their favorite brands. What are these brands doing right? Quite simply: They're paying attention, breaking some old "rules" of marketing, and taking action. We list 10 of their preferred brands here, in no particular order. Each snapshot is a small glimpse into how those brands are winning the hearts, minds, and wallets of Pivotals.

Nike

The athletic brand is more than 50 years old, but it remains young in spirit through constant innovation. It walks the walks when it comes to diversity, inclusion, and product customization—the Pivotal trifecta.

PROOF OF PURPOSE

In 2017, Nike released the Nike Pro Hijab, a hijab designed for female Muslim athletes. Though it generated controversial opinions, the Pro Hijab was authentic support of a generation pushing for equality. Nike is a brand that has consistently lived its story.

Pivotal marketing mogul Ziad Ahmed notes that, although brands can be "cringeworthy" in pandering to a younger audience, he felt Nike was one brand doing it right, particularly referring to their Nike Pro Hijab. "I like that brands are making efforts to be inclusive."

Ahmed's advice to brands striving for diversity? "It needs to look natural. It needs to look like America. Don't just check the boxes— that's not what society looks like."

Nike's recent "Equality" campaign encourages people to take the fairness and respect they see in sports and translate those values off the field. It is meant to inspire people to take action in their communities. As Nike has a long history of supporting causes, it owned the editorial authority to champion the message. (See Figure 7-1.)

At the center of the campaign is a short film featuring famous Nike athletes, including LeBron James, Serena Williams, Gabby Douglas, and others, using their voices to highlight the positive values of sports. The film, featuring a performance by Alicia Keys, ends with the line, "If we can be equals here, we can be equals everywhere."

PRODUCT PERKS

Nike's sneaker customization feature, NikeiD, allows consumers to design and order a unique shoe made to their specifications. Consid-

EQUALITY HAS NO BOUNDARIES.

Figure 7-1 Adapted from Nike's "Equality has no boundaries" campaign.

ering what we've found in previous chapters, it comes as no surprise that a visually focused application for creating one's own individualized merchandise is a hit with Pivotals. According to them, Nike makes apparel that's both stylish and comfortable.

"I recently designed and ordered my own shoes on Nike's website," said Grant, age 14. "I'm big into collecting sneakers."

CONSUMER CONNECTION

In a glowing example of communicating with Pivotals on their own terms, Nike dominates the social media sphere. Its strategy revolves around three main points.

First, Nike goes beyond selling sports. Its messaging focuses on a lifestyle and a vision for a better life. Powerful images of surfers hitting a massive wave focus on the athlete, not the product. Even though the Nike swoosh is always present, the athlete remains the hero. Nike is simply proud to be involved in the aspirational story.

Second, Nike creates a different persona for each sport. Much like Pivotals, Nike understands a soccer player possesses a different style than a basketball player. The imagery, language, and placement reflect this understanding.

How does Nike accomplish this artistry of balancing product promotion and organic content? That's where the third point comes into play: brand ambassadors. By bringing in both celebrity status athletes and emerging figures, Nike learns to speak the language through immersion. It doesn't predict or pontificate. Nike shuts up and listens.

Lululemon

With the Athleisure trend at peak popularity, Nike isn't the only brand finding success with Gen Z. Lululemon, the high-end athletic retailer, has mastered the balance between sweat and style.

PROOF OF PURPOSE

Not only does the brand produce fashionable, high-quality clothing, but it also aims to make a social impact both globally and locally. Lu-

Figure 7-2 Rendering of one of Lululemon's in-store yoga classes.

lulemon employs more than 1,600 influencers ("ambassadors")—comprised of athletes, trainers, yoga instructors, and inspirational people—to promote its approach to philanthropy and represent its brand.

Instead of traditional, expensive endorsements with high-profile athletes, the brand supports the philanthropic efforts of its ambassadors, who create communities and social impact programs. "Their agenda is to support your agenda," said Tyrone Beverly, a Lululemon brand ambassador.[7] Lululemon's goal is to foster authentic relationships through a grassroots approach while creating a community that rallies around social impact programs.

PRODUCT PERKS

"I really connect with them because I'm an active person," explained 17-year-old Maddie S. She added:

> I'm always running around, going to different school events, so I wear their clothing a lot. It's cute and it's really good quality. They came out with a line that glows in the dark so you can run at night. The message was that you can work out whenever, so there should be no excuses. I think that's motivational.

Teens' love of Lululemon proves that quality sometimes trumps price when the brand is a "status" symbol and helps them achieve their personal goals. While Ivivva, the sister brand of Lululemon aimed at tween/teen consumers, is slightly more affordable (although still averaging around $60 for a pair of athletic pants), Pivotals still embrace Lululemon as a favorite.

CONSUMER CONNECTION

Certainly having products in the trendy athleisure fashion space would give any brand a head start. But Lululemon doesn't stop there. The brand markets its products almost entirely through word of mouth and experiential, community-based events, setting them apart from louder, interruption-focused campaigns. For example, some Lululemon retail stores transform into free workout centers on the weekends or offer sunset yoga classes at local parks. (See Figure 7-2.)

Lululemon isn't just selling yoga pants; it's selling a healthier lifestyle and a more accepting community.

Target

Sometimes jokingly pronounced *Targét* (dating back to the 1960s, the pseudo-French pronunciation gives a nod to the store's up-to-date, boutique feel), this big-box store uses its army of "team members" and innovative checkout processes to, according to Target.com, "[o]ffer personal, easy and convenient options whenever and however you choose to shop."

However, those convenient options aren't the only reason Target continues to grow. From its community involvement to their affordability, Target is making waves with Pivotals.

PROOF OF PURPOSE

Outside the red doors, the company has a long history of giving back and supporting the communities in which it operates. In 2015, the company announced it had reached its goal of raising $1 billion for education in the United States and around the world.

With one of its core beliefs being "Celebrate Diversity and Inclusion," Target seeks to hire employees of diverse backgrounds and develops relationships with minority-owned suppliers. Additionally, those diverse employees receive growth and leadership opportunities throughout the entirety of their stay on the "Target Team."

PRODUCT PERKS

On the customer side, Target goes beyond selling products and makes concerted efforts to support Pivotals as they create their identity through clothing, entertainment, and home decor. The welcoming environment, award-winning mobile app Cartwheel, Dollar Spot deals, and, in some cases, a Starbucks by the entrance all create a winning environment for a generation focused on value and experience.

"This store makes me feel like I have my life together," admits Maddie, age 19. "I could be having the worst day and my friends and I will just take a trip to Target like it's a therapy session."

Figure 7-3   Rendering of a screenshot of an image of Alex Lee posted on Twitter.

Remember "Alex from Target," the unsuspecting, attractive young employee whose picture, taken and shared on Twitter by a young female customer, became an overnight sensation? (See Figure 7-3.) In less than 24 hours, he went from being a regular, relatively obscure teenager to being a top story on CNN! That may have been when teens first fell in love with Target.

That love affair continues today due to a concerted effort by the superstore to attract and retain Pivotal consumers. Each of Target's social media channels is full of culturally relevant, platform-appropriate content. On Instagram, for instance, Target acts as a "lifestyle curator," sharing stylized, aspirational product photos.[8] On Snapchat, Target uses geofilters around different holiday events, targeted around its physical stores to drive traffic and sales.

Target also recently announced its clothing collection, Art Class, designed for Generation Z with the creative help of 10 talented young influencers.[9] To develop the Art Class brand, Target did its homework and went right to the source, influential Gen Zers and their parents. While price is a main factor for parents, Pivotals piece together outfits in a way that expresses their individuality.[10] Target is the cross-section of both.

Apple

This brand almost requires little to no introduction. But for those who have been hiding under a rock, Apple is *the* smartphone/computer/ music player of choice for the identity-conscious Pivotal generation. From packaging to products to advertising, Apple keeps it simple and gives the user the freedom to build something meaningful.

PROOF OF PURPOSE

On the note of freedom, Apple was one of the first mega corporations to hire an openly gay CEO, Tim Cook. Cook praised Apple for being a company "that loves creativity and innovation and knows it can only flourish when you embrace people's differences."[11]

Interestingly, some of the same teens praising the brand also noted their hesitation in supporting a company so clearly monopolizing the industry. Apple is one of the biggest and most profitable companies in the world. Yet, there is no denying Apple's positive impact, from its simplistic and high-quality products to its environmentally friendly and forward-thinking policies.

PRODUCT PERKS

Pivotals surveyed in our study said their love of Apple is a result of reliable, easy-to-use products that are both stylish and necessary for them to function in their daily lives. As one teen phrased it, "Apple basically runs our world."

Angie's kids accused her of being stuck in the Dark Ages until she switched from an Android phone to an iPhone and from a PC laptop to a MacBook. They just couldn't imagine how she could operate without Apple at the center of her life.

This is why some are calling them iGen. The little "i" pays homage to the brand and indicates something made easy, from sharing photos and music to connecting with friends, getting real-time news, watching (or making) funny videos, and so on. Apple essentially provides everything at Gen Z's fingertips, all in sleek little packages that connect and work together.

The success of the iPod and subsequent models isn't attributed just to the quality of the device, either, but to the design. Steve Jobs, famous for his unbridled commitment to design and function, set a precedent for sleek and sophisticated devices that promote the desire to create. The perfect blank canvas.

CONSUMER CONNECTION

What's most interesting about Apple is its counterintuitive marketing approaches. You will never find Apple competing in a pricing battle or offering coupons or discounts. The brand doesn't create complicated ads detailing every product feature.

Instead, Apple engages customers on an emotional level. Using modern marketing methods, TV, Internet ads, print, and product placement, Apple sells the feeling of joy. Of fun and satisfaction. You will never see an Apple advertisement listing its features or battery life. Instead, the brand focuses on creating a feeling of mystery. It alludes to a life-changing product, generates hype, and, when it finally reveals the product, focuses on what *you* can do *with* the product, not what the *product* can do *for* you.

Netflix

What started as a mail-order DVD rental service has evolved into a video production and streaming giant. With original content, Netflix transformed the way teens view entertainment, and it's done so with a tight grasp on a worthwhile pursuit.

PROOF OF PURPOSE

Many companies pursue charitable ventures outside its company walls; philanthropies, foundations, and donations are common. But Netflix chose a new approach. It chose to focus internally on its greatest investment: its employees.

While many companies are catching on, Netflix was one of the first companies to offer flexible work hours and unlimited vacation time. In 2015, the company announced paid maternity and paternity leave for up to a year, giving parents time to bond with their children without worrying about income.

Netflix understands that to make the world a better place, it has to start from within. And tending to employees, making them feel understood and appreciated, is one of the best ways to create a lasting business.

PRODUCT PERKS

With social media elevating consumer conversations surrounding TV and pop culture, Netflix has inspired millions of young consumers to move away from cable and opt for a Netflix, Hulu, or HBO GO kind of life. Millennials were Cable-Cutters; Pivotals are Cable-Nevers.

With Gen Z, Netflix and binge watching are synonymous, propelling Netflix into "verb" territory (much like Google). Just don't say "Netflix and chill" without expecting a few sideways glances.[12]

CONSUMER CONNECTION

Additionally, Netflix "listens" to its users through user viewer profiles. Every interaction with the app yields better movie and show recommendations. As a bonus, by recommending lesser known shows, Netflix is able to purchase the rights to lower-profile and less expensive titles, keeping the streaming cost low.

The company has quickly taken away the "real-time" urgency from big networks, making all episodes available all the time, changing the conversation from "you missed out" to "you should get involved."

Starbucks

What is it about Starbucks that resonates so strongly with teens, especially when many don't even drink coffee yet?

The answer is simple: Starbucks is digital and mobile, offers relevant rewards, and creates an environment where teens want to be. The secret menu of unicorn and cotton candy frappuccinos is an added bonus!

PROOF OF PURPOSE

Most corporations of such epic proportion struggle to invest in each and every employee, but Starbucks tackled the puzzle head-on.

By paying for up to four years of college tuition at Arizona State University's online program, Starbucks supports its employees pursuing an education. The coffee brand also offers private health insurance to its employees.

Beyond its employees, Starbucks publically supports disadvantaged populations in its hiring practices, a cause Gen Z is particularly passionate about. Previous campaigns included pledging to employ 10,000 refugees by the year 2022 and 25,000 veterans and their spouses by the year 2025.

PRODUCT PERKS

Starbucks is the ultimate customizable brand. It's nearly impossible to get sick of the menu, as there are thousands upon thousands of potential drink combinations. Between its standard coffees, flavored lattes, tea-based drinks, and Frappuccinos, there's a drink for everyone. The brand regularly releases new innovations of classic coffee drinks and completely original beverages based on the season, flavor, and even color (pink drink!). Beverage personalization is expected rather than frowned upon, as it might be at a more standard coffeehouse.

Wherever you live, you're bound to find a Starbucks nearby. Plus, it's got fast service down to a science with its barista lineup, mobile order, and drive-through options. But if you aren't looking to grab your coffee and run, the stores are equipped with comfy chairs and free Wi-Fi to encourage in-store gatherings and meetings. Starbucks stores have evolved into a hangout location for young people as a result of the homey atmosphere, convenience, and accessibility. The brand name and logo carry a weight of their own. In fact, Starbucks has become practically synonymous with coffee ("I'm going to grab a Starbucks!").

CONSUMER CONNECTION

Starbucks has completely adapted to Pivotals' communication style and speaks their language: social media. The Starbucks Instagram account has more than 14 million followers, and teens are tagging the coffee company in their posts on a regular basis. Campaigns like Tweet-a-Coffee and the Starbucks app allow consumers to share coffee and connect with one another through social media.

It's rumored that by misspelling customers' names, Starbucks designed a low-key ad campaign to spread brand awareness. Thousands of tweets and Instagram photos include the Starbucks branding, and many mention the brand specifically. The quirky mistake is whimsical, fun, and a sneaky way to win over hearts. (See Figure 7-4.)

Figure 7-4   A rendering of a collage of one loyal customer's misspelled Starbucks cups.

In a more traditional approach, Starbucks also offers benefits for participating in the rewards program like free music and app downloads. The catch is that you must use the Starbucks app for your drinks to count toward the My Starbucks Rewards program. Scanners at Starbucks' registers read the barcodes on phone screens, so it is now a common sighting to see a customer reach for his or her phone instead of a wallet when paying for that tall skinny vanilla latte.

Chipotle

It's a rare victory to find a Chipotle that doesn't have a line all the way to the door, but don't be fooled because, with its assembly-line setup, you'll be at the front before you know it. Customized meals, efficient service, and affordable "Food with Integrity," contribute to Pivotals' love of this Tex-Mex chain.

PROOF OF PURPOSE

But "Food with Integrity" is more than just lip service or fleeting corporate initiative. Chipotle's philosophy is to always do better in terms of the food it buys: "Better-tasting, coming from better sources, better for the environment, better for the animals, and better for the farmers."

In spring 2017, Chipotle produced an unbranded video series called *RAD Lands* to teach kids about healthy eating. They show celebrity chefs and real kids—along with a healthy dose of animation—participating in cooking segments and talking about relevant topics such as what it's like to work on a farm.

In a March 2017 *Fortune* article, Chipotle's CMO and development officer, Mark Crumpacker, said: "This content reinforces ideas about the brand and makes [existing customers] more loyal. It doesn't mean that non-customers don't see those videos. But they speak to people that have a pre-existing relationship with Chipotle."

PRODUCT PERKS

Even a much-publicized *E. coli* breakout in 2016 couldn't keep teens away from Chipotle. Chipotle is Pivotals' second favorite food destination, second only to Starbucks.[13]

One survey respondent told us, "Chipotle makes up about a fourth of my weekly diet." Another said, "I get my money's worth. I'm full for about five hours after I eat there, and it's sooooo good!"

Today's teens are moving away from traditional fast food in search of healthier, more nutritious choices. In fact, being food aware is a growing trend with Pivotals—some calling them the second wave of "foodies." They want to know where their food comes from, increasingly demanding food with integrity. And, as it just so happens, that's Chipotle's slogan.

CONSUMER CONNECTION

Chipotle has a reputation for producing entertaining yet impactful nontraditional marketing content. Its 2013 award-winning animated short, *The Scarecrow*, showed how poorly other large restaurant chains processed food, and in 2011, the company produced *Back to the Start*, taking aim at highly industrialized food manufacturing.

The company also follows Pivotals' rules in social, posting channel-appropriate content that both inspires and entertains. "There is resistance to advertising," Crumpacker added. "This content gives you another way to engage with people."

With that kind of sincerity and authenticity, it is little wonder Chipotle is a favorite among young consumers.

Panera

Panera has a lot in common with Chipotle. In fact, the two brands often get mentioned in the same sentence when talking about the restaurants Pivotals love. Both fast-casual chains offer fresh and made-to-order options and are transparent about where their food comes from and how it's made. They're all about consumer trust.

PROOF OF PURPOSE

Panera's brand promise is "Food as It Should Be." It started in 2015 when Panera published a "No No List" of more than 80 ingredients—from acesulfame K to synthetic vanilla—that it was committed to removing from all of its food products by the end of 2016. Then, Panera's CEO posted a letter in *The New York Times* highlighting his commitment to healthier ingredients.

The brand's 2017 marketing campaign emphasized "100% Clean" ingredients. It was promoted through TV spots and billboards but also reached consumers directly by offering free samples and encouraging people to share their experiences and opinions on social media.

PRODUCT PERKS

Panera has earned its trust and brand love with Pivotals for more than its transparency, however. Did you know:

- Panera was once the largest supplier of free Wi-Fi in the United States, and one of the first companies to offer free Wi-Fi in all locations?
- Panera was the first company in the United States to voluntarily post calorie counts?
- Panera has a "hidden" menu? (That includes steak lettuce wraps—yum!)
- Panera donates all leftover food each day to local hunger relief agencies?

With teens spending more of their money on eating out than almost anything else, emphasizing choice and convenience—as well as "clean" food—is a clear formula for success.

CONSUMER CONNECTION

Over the years, Panera has invested heavily in utilizing technology to provide the most efficient quick-service experience. Both its mobile app and website allow consumers to order hours or days in advance, then come in at the requested time and grab their food from a Rapid Pick-Up shelf without having to wait. Through Panera's digital ordering system, users can customize their meals and save the customizations for future orders.

Dine-in customers can use the app and have the food delivered directly to their tables, and delivery is also available in select locations. In recent years, Panera has also added ordering kiosks in place of cashiers to reduce lines and simplify the ordering process. If there's anything you've learned about Pivotals, it's that they hate waiting!

Sephora

Cosmetic industry revenues were at an all-time high in 2016, due in no small part to the popularity of how-to beauty and makeup videos from social media influencers like Michelle Phan and Zoella. But with makeup readily available in almost every grocery store and drugstore, why is Gen Z making a special trip to Sephora?

PROOF OF PURPOSE

The beauty brand's social initiatives are comprised of three main campaigns: Sephora Accelerate, Classes for Confidence, and Sephora Stands Together.

Each year, Sephora Accelerate brings together beauty industry leaders to mentor 10 selected women on how to become successful beauty entrepreneurs, assisting with a fully fleshed-out business plan, grants, and meetings with potential venture partners. The program fosters female leadership in business, which is particularly important in the beauty industry since the majority of the consumers are women.

Sephora's Classes for Confidence partner with nonprofit organizations to offer free classes that "spread a message of attainable workplace beauty and confidence."[14] The classes provide instruction on how to cultivate a professional appearance for women looking to transition into the workplace.

For Sephora employees going through unexpected hardships, Sephora Stands Together provides short-term financial help. The company also promotes community causes, hosting an annual volunteer day at its headquarters, distribution centers, and retail locations.

PRODUCT PERKS

Sephora offers great products, which is an obvious must. But it goes deeper. Sephora stores are popular destinations among Pivotals, not only as a one-stop makeup shop—offering both a reasonably priced house brand and higher-end brands like Smashbox, Urban Decay, and Too Faced—but also as a fun and friendly place. It offers activities like custom makeovers and teen makeup classes, free for Beauty Insiders, Sephora's rewards program members.

In the "old days," shoppers basically had two options for purchasing beauty products: drugstores or high-end department stores. Nothing in between. Then, along comes an option in the middle: stores that offer lower-priced brands alongside more expensive, upscale brands. And even better, stores that allow customers to test the products before buying! No more second-guessing.

In addition, Sephora is an innovator in the beauty industry. Recognizing Pivotals' fascination with augmented reality, the company launched the first 3D augmented-reality mirror. (See Figure 7-5.) The mirror locates a user's facial features and applies eye shadow colors directly via a video feed from a camera. Shoppers can try out different shades and view themselves from different angles to see what looks best on them.

Figure 7-5 Adapted from Modiface's 3D augmented-reality mirror.

CONSUMER CONNECTION

Like most brands with Pivotal appeal, Sephora understands the value of being front and center with young consumers in social media: namely, Snapchat and more recently Kik, a mobile messaging app. The company recently announced its use of chatbots that lead users through friendly prompts to provide custom tips and product suggestions—then allow shoppers to click-to-shop without ever having to leave the Kik app. (See Figure 7-6.)

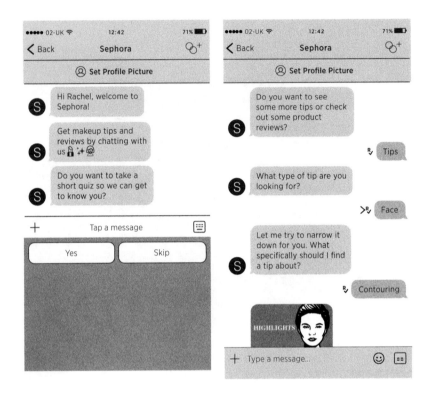

Figure 7-6 A rendering of Sephora's chatbot in action on Kik.

Chick-fil-A

Chick-fil-A is one of the most successful fast-food chains in the country, and, additionally, its franchises cost very little to open.[15] In 2016, Chick-fil-A boasted an 18 percent sales increase and a reputation as the fifth fastest growing chain.[16] Its Eat Mor Chikin cow campaign is still running strong after more than 20 years. Tasty chicken sandwiches, waffle fries, and polite Southern-style service . . . what more could Pivotals want in a family-friendly fast-food restaurant?

PROOF OF PURPOSE

Chick-fil-A hit a reputational road bump in 2012 when its CEO, Dan Cathy, admitted the company supported "the biblical definition of marriage" and opposed same-sex marriages. The liberal-leaning, equality-focused Pivotal generation joined others in speaking up in protest.

However, like all great brands, the company has since acted in favor of modern consumer expectations, downplaying religion and politics, and embracing a more inclusive culture. Operators are encouraged to get involved in their communities, focusing on youth and education.

"We are not a political organization. We are not a social change organization. We are a restaurant. . . . We want Chick-fil-A to be for everyone," said David Farmer, Chick-fil-A's vice president of menu strategy and development.[17]

PRODUCT PERKS

Chick-fil-A's menu has evolved as well. To compete head-to-head with fast-casual favorites like Chipotle and distance itself from fast-food burger chains like McDonald's, Chick-fil-A updated its menu to include healthier options, including grilled chicken nuggets and a kale-based "superfood side."

Chick-fil-A also is known for exceeding customer expectations, even down to the special little details, like tables set with fresh flowers, polite employees ("It's my pleasure" used in place of "You're welcome") and using names instead of ticket numbers when orders are ready. This likely appeals to Pivotals' more traditional values.

CONSUMER CONNECTION

A section on Chick-fil-A wouldn't be complete without mentioning how it handles grand openings. When the company opens a new restaurant, it reaches out to its most loyal customers, inviting them to a free preopening meal. Attendees at the events receive coupons for 10 free sandwiches, and one lucky winner (out of the first 100 customers) wins Chick-fil-A for a year. These grand openings are so popular that fans of all ages will travel long distances and even camp

Figure 7-7 A rendering of a Chick-fil-A grand opening.

out in Chick-fil-A parking lots to be part of the adventure. (See Figure 7-7.)

EPIC BRAND FAILS

Pivotals are ideal fans. They're vocal, public, and passionate—the perfect brand representative. But on the downside, if you swing for the fences with Pivotals, and they don't like what you're selling, you are in for a world of hurt.

The following brands are great examples of big swings and misses. They tried to speak the Pivotal language and failed, and thanks to social media, they failed on an epic scale.

Thankfully, the following missteps have more to do with poor strategy than bad luck; so learn from their mistakes and still swing for that home run.

Pepsi

Don't patronize Gen Z. As Pepsi learned, they get really pissed off when you do!

—THOMAS KOULOPOULOS, "WATCH HEINEKEN SCHOOL
PEPSI ON HOW TO ADVERTISE TO GEN Z
(IT'S A LESSON FOR EVERY BRAND)"[18]

In early 2017, Pepsi unveiled a controversial new ad as part of its Live for Now campaign. The commercial starred Kendall Jenner as a fashion model in the middle of a photo shoot during a protest (specific cause unclear) on the street outside.

Motivated by the sultry glance of a handsome protester, the model rips off her blonde wig, runs out of her shoot and joins the crowd of perfectly cast "diverse" individuals. Not content to merely march, she grabs a Pepsi and offers it to a somber police officer as a type of peace offering. He gladly accepts it and smiles, the crowd breaks out in cheers, high-fives, and hugs, and all is once again right with the world.

Unfortunately, the intended audience, Pivotals, didn't agree.

Almost immediately, the ad was accused of being "tone deaf" and unrealistic, trivializing the Black Lives Matter movement and using social justice to make a profit. Also, the imagery was eerily similar to photos of Ieshia Evans protesting against police brutality in Baton Rouge several months before.

The backlash was loud and swift. Some consumers called for firing the team responsible for the spot. Dr. Martin Luther King Jr.'s daughter even scorned the ad. Ultimately, Pepsi pulled the ad and issued a public apology.

"Pepsi was trying to project a global message of unity, peace and understanding. Clearly we missed the mark, and we apologize," Pepsi wrote in a statement. "We did not intend to make light of any serious issue. We are removing the content and halting any further rollout. We also apologize for putting Kendall Jenner in this position."

So much is wrong with this spot that it's hard to pinpoint how it could have been remedied. But we have a few ideas.

First, capitalizing on social unrest and politically charged issues is unwise for a brand with no background or editorial authority in the conversation. That was its first mistake. However, if Pepsi genuinely wanted to take a stand on the issue of racial injustice, casting a well-known activist would have been a better choice than Kendall Jenner.

Second, Gen Z wants to see reality reflected in advertising. Do people smile and enjoy Pepsi in the middle of a protest? Do protesters break out in jovial song and dance when surrounded by police?

Had Pepsi shared this spot with a focus group of Pivotal consumers, it never would have seen the light of day.

That said, Pepsi did the right thing by seeing the error of its ways and not only issuing a public apology but also quickly pulling the spot. And Pepsi, an otherwise well-regarded brand, probably won't suffer long-term damage with Pivotals from just one (albeit epic) blunder.

Abercrombie & Fitch

Speaking of tone deaf.

Remember when then CEO of Abercrombie & Fitch, Michael Jeffries, defended the company's position of excluding certain customers? In a 2006 interview with Salon, he said, "We go after the attractive all-American kid with a great attitude and a lot of friends. A lot of people don't belong [in our clothes], and they can't belong. Are we exclusionary? Absolutely."

Or how about when asked why A&F refused to carry women's clothing over a size 10, he said, "Good-looking people attract other good-looking people, and we want to market to cool, good-looking people . . . we don't market to anyone other than that."

In addition to those two PR fiascos, you also probably remember when A&F got sued over refusing to hire a 17-year-old Muslim girl who wore a headscarf to her job interview. The list goes on.

Abercrombie & Fitch clearly missed the memo about Pivotals valuing equality and inclusion and wanting to see real people reflected in advertising. That ultimately hurt the brand in the form of public backlash and declining sales.

The good news is that the brand learned a very important lesson and is attempting a turn around to "reflect the character, charisma and confidence of today's consumer while honoring the brand's 125-year heritage as a quality, casual and distinctively American luxury brand."

In the years since, Abercrombie & Fitch has made significant strides to rebrand and win back alienated consumers. The first step was firing Jeffries. It was also getting rid of oversexualized images of scantily clad models and replacing them with models actually wearing the brand's clothing.

Now targeting the slightly older 18- to 25-year-old demographic, Abercrombie's advertising focuses less on the unattainable and more on refined, realistic portrayals. Their 2017 redesign featured open, transparent storefronts, private fitting room suites, lighter fragrances, and warmer decor in an effort to evolve into a more approachable, personalized brand. Time will tell whether A&F can make a comeback. (For the record, we hope it does!)

GLIMMERS OF GREATNESS

While we covered only 10 brands, plenty of brands are still taking the right steps toward meeting Pivotals' preferences. Brands using IRL (in real life) tactics consistently win with Pivotals by setting themselves apart from digitally focused brands and giving their young consumers something to talk about. Pivotals are so accustomed to digital pervading every aspect of their lives that a real-life interaction seems novel and relieving.

From implementing experiential marketing and showcases to reverting back to older tactics like direct mail, brands pursuing Pivotals are going all-out in their approaches. Some, like Zipcar, are even infiltrating college campuses, using creative guerilla marketing tactics to gain awareness and attention.

CASE STUDY

Who: Zipcar

What: The world's leading car-sharing network went straight to the source, college campuses, in an effort to engage its new target market, Gen Z, in an authentic, offline environment.

How: The strategy included a number of unexpected and innovative tactics employed on college campuses, which tend to be heavily concentrated with Gen Zers. Through the human-powered advertising service, NOMAD, student backpacks became moving billboards that inspired face-to-face conversations. Themed emoji cars decaled with life-size versions of the digital icons encouraged students to get creative with their destinations. Additionally, a so-called Zipmadness activation played off March Madness by turning Zipcar parking spots into miniature basketball courts.

Impact: Zipcar's creativity gave Gen Z a tangible way to engage with the brand in the real world. Student members employed the company's services in new ways; for instance, a car that featured heart and moon emojis encouraged date nights. Not only that, Zipcar implemented ways for Pivotals to interact with the brand in the context of their own schools and communities. Zipmadness became a campus conversation topic and interactive experience, and backpack advertising led to increased campus engagement.

"The reaction from Gen Z blew us out of the water," said Kate Pope Smith, Zipcar director of integrated marketing. "They really seemed to have a desire for doing business with real people who offered a very customized and personalized brand experience."

IRL Experiences Foster Connections

Events like music festivals and brand activations provide Pivotals with not only memorable in-person entertainment but also shareable social media content to benefit their personal brands. Marketers value branded experiences for these same reasons: They resonate with Pivotals in a palpable, personal way that digital advertising cannot. Pivotals don't want to be sold to; they want to interact. Pivotals who immerse themselves in these events develop these deeper connections with the brands and become more brand loyal as a result.

According to The Pineapple Agency, an experiential activation "enables the company to show how they bring a much bigger value by immersing the audience and making them a part of the process, rather than the value produced by the product or service alone."[19]

By hosting a branded activation with photo opportunities and a unique experience, marketers hand the tools over to Gen Z and essentially allow them to do the work. Pivotals benefit from the experience and want to post about it on social media, while brands provide the novelty and humanization of a live event and receive word-of-mouth promotion in return.

CASE STUDY

Who: TAKE5

What: To introduce a new generation to the candy bar brand, parent company Hershey (a former Barkley client) knew traditional advertising wasn't the answer. Instead, it needed to create word of mouth through unique, share-worthy sampling experiences representing the brand. For its first such experience, the brand chose the granddaddy of all festivals, South by Southwest (SXSW).

How: Celebrating the convergence of the interactive, film, and music industries (three things Gen Z loves!), SXSW is the premier destination for discovering new things, which is why it's also extremely crowded with brands vying for young consumers' attention. To stand out, TAKE5 created an experience specifically relevant to SXSW: the TAKE5 Swag Exchange.

The TAKE5 Swag Exchange provided a creative solution to a common problem at large festivals: swag overload. The Swag Exchange, located in one of the main SXSW hotspots throughout the festival, used a custom algorithm based on supply and demand to calculate the daily value of each piece of swag. For five straight days, attendees visited the TAKE5 Swag Exchange to swap, trade, and exchange swag they didn't want for more desirable items (like gift certificates to popular restaurants and VIP tickets to festival events). After that, they stayed to enjoy great music, a TAKE5 GIF booth, and plenty of other picture-worthy fun. After the festival, TAKE5 donated all unused swag to local Austin nonprofits.

Brand ambassadors drove attendance to the Swag Exchange by passing out 150,000 TAKE5 candy bars with stickers directing them to the Swag Exchange. The brand also invested in geo-targeted content on Instagram, Twitter, and Facebook, while Instagram influencers leveraged the TAKE5 social channels to amplify the event to a national audience.

Impact: More than 2,700 festival attendees, which was more than double the expected number, attended the Swag Exchange. They brought almost 6,000 pieces of swag, and people stayed for an average of 30 minutes. The TAKE5 Swag Exchange social content efforts achieved an 18 percent engagement rate, with paid and organic efforts generating 32.7 million impressions during the festival.

Print Makes a Comeback

Everything old is new again at some point, right? Believe it or not, print media and direct mail are actually making a comeback with Pivotals.

According to Mintel's 2016 report, "Marketing to the iGeneration," brands may be missing an opportunity if they're ignoring snail mail, since 83 percent of Pivotals love getting stuff in the mail.[20] Direct mail has become a novelty, so it has the potential to stand out.

When Phil Gilliam, cofounder of *BYou* magazine, decided to start a print publication for young girls, his peers thought he was crazy. Who still reads print in this digital age? After trying and failing to market to the moms who would be paying for the magazine, Gilliam shifted his efforts to reach 8- to 16-year-old girls themselves and discovered that Pivotals love receiving mail. After all, it's a reliable, personalized piece of entertainment. Though direct mail may not be a new tactic, it is certainly underutilized for the Gen Z market.

A generic advertisement will not be successful as Pivotal-targeted direct mail. Include the piece in something they're already excited about, like a magazine or subscription box. Mintel's 2016 "Marketing to the iGeneration" report suggests using catalogs as lifestyle magazines with a companion online aspect to increase brand loyalty.[21]

"Think of the direct mail piece as a live version of a digital advertisement," explained Gilliam.

The tactile quality of print media engages Pivotals' desire for a sensory, physical experience. Since they are so used to digital media, Gen Zers view print as "non-traditional marketing."[22] Imagine that!

A dynamic offer such as a unique experience, a free preview, behind-the-scenes access, or something special intrigues Pivotals and gets them to act rather than just throw the piece away. In fact, direct mail has a longer shelf life than digital advertisements, as it will remain until someone physically throws it away.

Interestingly, print appeals most to Hispanic Pivotals at 66 percent, followed closely by African Americans and Asians, at 64 percent and 62 percent, respectively, according to the second wave of the "ThinkNow Gen We Are Gen Z Report," by ThinkNow Research and Sensis Agency.[23]

WHAT IT ALL MEANS

From day one, Pivotals have been trained in the art of empowered consumerism. They know what they want, how to get it, and who to get it from. They see their own needs and preferences clearly and, coincidentally, can sense the needs in others. Driven by the needs of others and themselves, Pivotals are becoming the most influential group of consumers the world has ever known.

In the wake of empowered consumers, marketers are forced into uncharted territories, which many find uncomfortable. But not too long ago, we were confused by Millennials too, and while we can't claim to fully understand them now, we were able to adapt. We learned to embrace the participation economy, engage with consumers, and create brand partners. We did it then, and we can do it now.

It's time to take another huge leap forward with Pivotals. Like nervous parents, it's a little like handing over the keys to a recently licensed teen. Risky? A bit. But a necessary step on the path forward. It starts with putting Brand Me first, listening to support their desires, and helping them connect with the world around them.

As we've shown, some brands are already well on their way, while some still have a long way to go. Others may never get there. Change is hard; the resilient and flexible will see their reward.

■   ■   ■

KEY TAKEAWAYS

■ **Pivotals aren't just buying what you do. They are buying into why you do it.** Brands with the courage to stand for something will create emotional connections that foster brand affinity with Pivotals.

■ **While brand loyalty may be on the decline, it's not because Pivotals can't be loyal. It's because most brands haven't yet earned that loyalty.** Pivotals go where they get the most value, so brands that want Pivotals' loyalty must meet their price and quality expectations in addition to supporting their goals.

■ **Real-life experiences resonate with Pivotals in a palpable, personal way that digital advertising cannot.** Pivotals benefit from the experience and post about it on social media, while brands provide the novelty and humanization of a live event and receive word-of-mouth promotion in return.

■ **Direct mail has become a novelty, so it has the potential to stand out.** The tactile quality of print media engages Pivotals' desire for a sensory, physical experience.

■ **If your brand becomes a verb, you win.**

WHAT'S NEXT?

We aren't called FutureCast for nothing. Looking ahead is what we do. We have a point of view—based on reams of primary and secondary research, data, and analytics referenced throughout this book—about how great brands can future-proof themselves by harnessing the power of the Pivotal Generation, the most influential and sophisticated consumer group we've ever seen. Leaders who understand that progress requires change and that change requires courage will pave the way. Leaders like yourselves.

Most of this book has been dedicated to understanding and marketing to Pivotals today, but we want to conclude with predictions for the future: three key considerations as you position your brand in the years to come.

Here we go.

■　■　■

YOUTH CULTURE INFLUENCES ALL GENERATIONS

Today more than ever, youth culture permeates mainstream attitudes. Both market trends and consumer purchasing behavior respond to the shift in attitudes and beliefs. As early adopters of digital, social, and mobile trends, younger consumers create an overarching mindset that determines brand health and financial performance. Their desires and behaviors influence the way companies operate all over the world. As their influence flows up the generational line, it's essential to understand how teens think and behave.

Recently, FutureCast partnered with Barkley, our parent company, and The Cambridge Group to reflect on what we've learned about Millennials after a decade of research and how it extends to the general population between the ages of 15 and 65. Through our research of young consumers' behaviors and attitudes, six mindsets emerged that highlight how young consumers, as a whole, influence consumer spending and behaviors across all generations. The biggest takeaway is that youth culture acts as a canary in the coal mine to predict broader consumer culture trends.

Throughout the following section, any reference to the term "Youth Mindset" isn't reserved for Pivotals. Instead, the Youth Mindset describes the mindsets among consumers up to age 65 who have been *most influenced* by the attitudes and beliefs of younger consumers.

So on that note, not all of the following examples are Pivotal-focused. Instead, we intend to highlight the best examples of each of mindset, regardless of target audience, to paint the best picture of the Youth Mindset.

Social Circle: Is My Brand Part of Cultural Conversations?

When brand marketers hear the word "social," they most often think of social media. Yes, social media is a powerful tool, but it's just *one* part of the overall *social circle:* the modern consumer's team of advisors. The social circle is the most influential pillar in the Youth Mindset. These advisors come from all over, ranging from social media networks to personal connections. Brands that build a strong social circle can tap into their micro influencers (the top identified brand advisors) to create an army of vocal brand fans. The bigger the social circle is, the greater the word of mouth and the better profit potential.

Trader Joe's is one of the most successful brands today when it comes to activating a consumer's social circle. Even a whisper of good news spreads like wildfire through the network. Before Trader Joe's opens a new location, consumers hype up one another in anticipation. Consider Trader Joe's position: It provides shoppers with the tools to create a shared experience with their friends and family, and its social circle is just one of their tools.

Self: Does My Brand Create an Emotional Connection with the Consumer?

Emotion is a powerful force. In fact, consumers with a strong emotional bond to a brand are less likely to stray. Building emotional connections is difficult, but it's ultimately the key to exceptional brand performance.

When consumers realize that a brand understands them on a personal level—and provides opportunities for greater self-exploration—they're much more likely to feel a sense of loyalty to that brand. Those emotionally bonded brands are afforded flexible pricing points and steady demand. This emotional mindset mirrors a current trend: Utility is the new currency. Brands helping consumers have more fulfilling lives are winning big.

Red Bull is a perfect example. Now the most popular energy drink in the world, Red Bull cultivated a brand identity based on adventure, excitement, and risk taking. When you drink Red Bull, you demonstrate your audacity to push the limits. To excel. From sponsoring extreme sports enthusiasts and athletes, to creating unique sports and events, to evoking emotions in unconventional ways, Red Bull is all about creating fan-centered experiences.

Innovative: Is My Brand Constantly Improving and Reinventing Itself?

Technology is making it easier for individuals and companies to innovate. An advance in one industry changes in another expectations about what is possible or expected. Modern consumers want the novelty, efficiency, and effectiveness that comes with product innovation, as well as the ways brands can make their lives easier, faster, and just generally better. New products, beta tests, and large jumps in tech attract interest and engagement across generations.

While Google is one of the best performing companies in the world, it remains committed to a start-up mentality. It creates agile and responsive teams and processes to keep innovation and new ideas center stage. The company has weekly TGIF meetings, where all Googlers seek input and conversation from every level of the workforce. The Google campuses themselves are set up to promote this connected mentality and entrepreneurialism. Google seeks out the best and the brightest from all walks of life and lets them do what they do best.

Google wasn't the first search engine, as Susan Wojcicki, Google's senior VP of advertising, notes, but it rose to the top by "working quickly, learning faster and taking its next steps based on data."[1] The company still operates this way, which has allowed it to remain successful and relevant years later. The role innovation plays in creating brand preference is important. Based on our research, we'd expect to see this increase accelerate. Consumers will pay a modest premium for brands that better meet their need-states.

Trusted: Is My Brand Remarkably Consistent?

Consumers today have more access to brands than ever before. Keeping secrets and important information hidden behind red tape is no longer an option. Building trust is the first step to any great relationship, and the most trusted brands are transparent, authentic, and altruistic.

FedEx is a top example of a brand that has earned consumer trust by consistently delivering on brand promises. According to Netbase, a social analytics platform, FedEx consistently earns the highest Net Sentiment score compared to its competitors. This is due in large part to FedEx delivering on its promises by removing friction from a traditionally stress-laden process.

Purposeful: Does My Brand Add Good to Society?

Youth Mindset consumers are looking for brands with a humanitarian approach to business. Today, brands must acknowledge that the triple bottom line—people, planet, and profit—is alive and well. Businesses cannot exist in a modern market if they focus solely on profit and loss statements. Consumers look to their favorite brands to help them make their communities better and to provide them with the tools they need to impact their world.

Blake Mycoskie is often credited with propelling the buy-one/give-one business model into the mainstream marketplace. When Mycoskie founded Tom's Shoes, his goal was to create a for-profit business that had major environmental, economic, and community impact. Not only did he succeed, he set a new standard for businesses across the board. Tom's Shoes was ranked the highest for Purpose in our Youth Mindset study, and what surprised us most is how that ranking was high across all generations (Pivotals, Millennials, Gen X, and Boomers). Brands committed to more than just their bottom line achieve success in connecting with Youth Mindset consumers.

Accessible: Is My Brand Hyperuseful and Hyperconvenient?

Accessibility is crucial. Youth Mindset consumers look for products and services that remove frustration and friction, easily fit into their lives, and address their various needs. And accessibility isn't confined to physical presence; consumers today are looking for access to brands across both physical *and* digital channels and for a seamless transition between the two. This all boils down to one big idea: Useful is the new cool.

Amazon is an extremely accessible brand. It created one of the biggest retail channels to date with no physical locations (although, for the record, that will be changing soon). Ordering online is now as easy as typing in what you are looking for (or browsing through the recommendations), clicking buy, and waiting for your package to arrive in two days. The Amazon Effect is the impact on consumer expectations as access to products or services increases. Amazon has set the bar higher than ever before in terms of convenience and immediacy.

GLOBAL BRANDS WILL HAVE AN ADVANTAGE

The World Wide Web made the whole world feel quite a bit smaller. As a result, the Pivotal Generation is truly a global generation. No longer restricted by the confines of geography, many Pivotals interact daily with peers from other countries. Faraway places don't seem so far away with Snapchat, Periscope, and other online platforms creating windows into global issues without the hindrances of media biases or geography.

In fact, because of their desire to get closer to their friends around the world, more than 50 percent of Pivotal college students have traveled abroad before their senior year, according to MediaVillage.[2] As a result, Pivotals don't harbor the same biases of older generations, which works to their advantage globally. They want acceptance, equality, diversity, and connection with their peers worldwide, and they hold their favorite brands to these same standards. A brand's reputation and image matter to Gen Z, not just here at home but also around the world.

Global brands will prevail in the coming years, especially since nearly half of Millennials (and likely even more Pivotals) expect to live and work abroad at some point in the future.[3] Distant countries influence our everyday lives, from Chinese-built phones to Ethiopian restaurants. In fact, due to today's rapid technological advancements, these young generations have access to a wealth of information. They are more informed and well versed on current issues than the youth of the past, resulting in a worldwide presence that is not to be underestimated.

CONSCIOUS CAPITALISM

We've talked about Proof of Purpose—that Pivotals aren't just buying *what* you do; they're buying into *why* you do it. For the activism-oriented Pivotal Generation, "conscious capitalist" brands will win. Conscious capitalist brands believe corporate performance is directly tied to advancing the quality of life around the world.

But don't get conscious capitalism confused with corporate social responsibility (CSR). CSR is just *one* element of conscious capitalism. Whereas CSR centers around companies' commitment to improve community well-being through discretionary business practices and/or corporate contributions, conscious capitalism is about companies putting higher values at the center of *everything* they do and creating shared value for everyone involved: employees, consumers, investors, suppliers, communities, and the planet. In other words, "doing good" and creating shared value is in the DNA of the company: It's business as usual, not an add-on.

The Ben & Jerry's brand has always been popular for its delicious and creatively monikered ice creams, but another major aspect of the brand is its commitment to create linked prosperity for everyone connected to the business, from employees, to farmers, to customers, to neighbors. The mission of the brand is focused on three key components:

1. **Product mission:** To make fantastic ice cream—for its own sake
2. **Economic mission**: To manage the company for sustainable financial growth
3. **Social mission:** To use the company in innovative ways to make the world a better place

Ben & Jerry's flexed its brand authority regarding these missions when it took a public stand with the Black Lives Matter movement (witnessed on all of its owned media) at the same time it launched its newest line of flavors to get the greatest amount of earned coverage possible. Rather than making a flavor named for the cause, as it has done in the past on previous social issues, the brand expressed support through a thoroughly well-written piece published to its website. It was clear the brand understood the entirety of the issue and acted accordingly in a way that was aligned with its purpose to achieve effective cultural currency.

As we outlined in our first book *Marketing to Millennials*, Millennials led the way for conscious capitalism. And as Millennials and Pivotals become the business leaders of tomorrow, their commitment to equality and social justice will fuel the demand for conscious capitalism as the required business practice for companies around the world.

Additionally, Pivotals are more likely than older generations to want to work for companies that try to make a positive difference in the world, and 72 percent of Generation Z will seek work that will make a difference and positively impact society.[4] Companies that demonstrate a true commitment to making a lasting difference in the world ultimately will attract the top Pivotal talent—yet another financial reason to embrace the four tenets of conscious capitalism as outlined by Conscious Capitalism, Inc.:[5]

1. **Higher purpose:** Pursuing a higher purpose beyond profit seeking
2. **Stakeholder orientation:** Generating value for all stakeholders and not just shareholders
3. **Conscious leadership:** Leaders who care about the higher purpose and stakeholder well-being
4. **Conscious culture:** Creating a more humanistic environment based on trust, authenticity, and transparency

DISRUPTIVE TECH OF TOMORROW

In a few short years, terms like "chatbots," "AI," and the "Internet of Things" (IoT) will be outdated. We're quickly moving into an age of previously improbable technology. Self-driving and flying cars. Brain implants to restore movement after paralysis. Face-detecting systems that authorize payments. Commercial trips to the moon. Universal translation in mobile devices. The world is both expanding in reach and shrinking in barriers.

Courtesy of advancing tech, the entire job market will look different than it does today, and Pivotals will become increasingly nimble in response. The good news: They're ready for it. But are the rest of us?

"We're in for a wave of economic disruption the likes of which we've never seen," says Mark Logan, senior vice president of innovation at Barkley. "In the next couple of decades, a significant percentage of today's jobs will be replaced by artificial intelligence (AI) and robotics."

At the same time new technologies make life more convenient by anticipating our needs and tailoring goods and services to our desires and personalities, it may make earning a living more challenging. Logan expects these trends will further exacerbate and accelerate wealth inequality.

"The pace of change we're about to see is too rapid to be easily absorbed. By some estimates, we're about to lose 50 percent of jobs in the next three decades. That's too many people to retrain for new jobs," Logan predicts.

Until then, we will continue to be amazed by shiny-new-penny technologies like virtual reality (VR). As VR becomes commonplace and the technology continues to improve in the next few years, we'll see an explosion of VR entertainment and immersive cinema options.

"If we think all of our social-media–induced ills are an issue now, just wait until we're spending hours immersed in virtual reality," says Logan.

Another prediction? As we become more and more immersed in technology, *non*tech activities, relationships, and spaces will become a new measure of the elite. Karen Faith, director of empathy and intelligence at Barkley, anticipates that just as those who don't have to do hard physical labor pay trainers to work their bodies, those with the time and freedom to step away from tech for an hour, a day, or a week will be considered the most exclusive, privileged group.

"We will have special Internet-disabled rooms for meetings without surveillance. We will have friendships that are prized because they are not logged online or do not operate text-only. Writers and speakers who can connect emphatically will be unicorns. But for the masses, most of this will be inaccessible," says Faith. "It's not more data we need, but more wisdom, insight, and clarity."

As technology shakes the world, how will your brand respond? Will you crumble or absorb the shock? Are you prepared to make massive shifts in business? Disruption is coming, and those willing to adapt will remain strong.

WHAT ARE YOU WAITING FOR?

By reading this book, you've made an investment in understanding this generation—what makes them tick, how they think and behave, and what they expect from brands. You've learned to win with this generation, as well as surefire ways to lose. What you take from this book is up to you, but if nothing else, we hope you've developed a deep appreciation for the ambitious, brilliant, Pivotal generation. We predict they will change the world for the better, and we look forward to watching it all unfold.

■ ■ ■

KEY TAKEAWAYS

- **Young consumers, as a whole, are influencing consumer spending and behaviors across all generations, via what we call the "Youth Mindset."** The six mindsets—social circle, self, innovative, trusted, purposeful, and accessible—will be what drives brand performance across industry verticals.

- **Global brands will prevail in the coming years.** The Pivotal generation is already a global generation, and, considering how strongly they value equality, connection, and technology, global brands are already poised to supersede national brands.

- **Pivotals are most interested in conscious capitalist brands, which believe corporate performance is directly tied to advancing the quality of life around the world.**

- **Enabled by technology, humans will, in a few decades, have enhanced control of nearly every aspect of our lives.** Modern brands must not only keep pace with technological advancements in such a rapidly evolving market but also stay *at least* one step ahead of consumer needs and expectations.

APPENDIX:
MAINTAIN COPPA COMPLIANCE

Disclaimer: **We're marketers, not lawyers.** So the following is meant as a word of caution, not as legal advice. That said, a book about marketing to Gen Z would be incomplete without mentioning the guidelines that govern marketing to the youngest of this generation, those under the age of 13.

As we've mentioned, Gen Z learned to swipe before they could even speak. They've never known a world without unprecedented access to information online. Likewise, as the world becomes increasingly digital, it's easier than ever for brands to communicate directly with specific consumer segments, including children under 13. Through websites, mobile apps, Internet-enabled gaming devices, and even connected toys and other Internet of Things devices, there are countless opportunities to connect with and collect personal information from children, tweens, and teens. And, as every parent will tell you, that's scary.

That's where the Children's Online Privacy Protection Act (COPPA) comes in. Enacted by Congress in 1998 and enforced by the Federal Trade Commission (FTC), COPPA is designed to protect children's privacy and safety online and puts parents in control over the information that companies (and other operators of commercial websites and/or online services) can collect from their kids online. Personal information like full name, home or physical address, email address or screen name, phone number, geo-location data, Social Security number, and even photos, videos or other files containing the child's image or voice. Even if providing their personal information is voluntary, it's always a no-no without parental consent.

Complying with COPPA includes several required actions, such as (but not limited to) prominently posting clear and comprehensive online privacy policies; providing a direct notice to parents and obtaining verifiable parental consent before collecting personal information from children; and maintaining the confidentiality, security, and integrity of that information.

Technology has changed a lot since COPPA's early days, and the FTC has updated its guidelines accordingly. So yes, that means COPPA extends to social media and mobile. For instance, if your target audience is under the age of 13, you are forbidden from integrating your social media platforms into your website. It would also be unwise to target social networks that don't use age-gates (requiring users to verify they are 13 or older), such as Twitter. It's always better to err on the safe side.

The same is true for sweepstakes and contests. States including Maine and California actually have laws that govern the collection of information from people under 18, so always do your homework before implementing sweepstakes and contests aimed at younger consumers.

Again, to ensure compliance, we recommend visiting the Federal Trade Commission (FTC) website at www.ftc.gov and consulting with your legal team. Violations can result in harsh penalties for brands—even brands like Disney aren't immune (Disney paid a $3 million settlement in 2011, the largest COPPA fine to date)—so maintaining compliance is not only a sound business decision; it's the right thing to do.

AFTERWORD

Pivotals will grow to become the most powerful consumer cohort in the market before we know it. They are already well on their way. Now is the time for marketers to prepare for the changing landscape that will result from these young consumers' ideals and expectations.

At Barkley and FutureCast, our journey to become the most informed agency in the United States on the attitudes and behaviors of emerging consumer groups started with a comprehensive study of Millennials in 2011. Through a partnership with The Boston Consulting Group and Service Management Group, our initial research study was the largest of its kind, leading to our first report, called "American Millennials: Deciphering the Enigma Generation." Since then, we have published dozens of reports, spoken around the world on the topic, and written two books: *Marketing to Millennials*, and *Millennials with Kids*.

Now, we turn our attention to Gen Z. Our initial report, published in 2017, "Getting to Know Gen Z: How the Pivotal Generation Is Different from Millennials," laid the groundwork for what we have covered thoroughly in this book: the outlooks, values, and preferences of tomorrow's most influential consumers.

All of this was done with one major goal in mind: to uncover deep insights and actionable steps to ensure our clients were able to modernize their brands for the future.

Publishing a book of this significance is no small feat. The outcome is a remarkable reflection of the dedication and hard work of Jeff

Fromm, Angie Read, and their team. They have incredible tenacity, and an ability to understand and answer the needs of not only our clients, but marketers and advertisers at large.

Thank you for reading this book. We hope it will prove to be a valuable source of insight and information as you prepare both your business and brand for the future.

Jeff King
CEO, Barkley

ENDNOTES

INTRODUCTION

1   Jeremy Finch, "What Is Generation Z, and What Does It Want?" *Fast Company*, May 4, 2015, http://www.fastcoexist.com/3045317/what-is-generation-z-and-what -does-it-want

2   "Activities of Kids and Teens-US," Mintel Reports, November 2013.

3   Our calculations are based on data from 2015 USDA child expenditures, 2016 US Census data, and 2016 Bureau of Labor Statistics consumer expenditure data. Contact authors for a copy of our analysis.

METHODOLOGY

1   Source: Barkley Inc. and FutureCast, LLC., "Getting to Know Gen Z: How the Pivotal Generation is Different from Millennials," 2017.

CHAPTER 1

1   "Hello, My Name Is. . ." United States Census Bureau, December 15, 2016, https://www.census.gov/library/visualizations/2016/comm/cb16-tps154 _surnames_top15.html

2   Sandra L. Colby and Jennifer M. Ortman, The Baby Boom Cohort in the United States: 2012–2060, May 2014, http://www.census.gov/prod/2014pubs/p25-1141 .pdf

3   Mario Carrasco, "3 Reasons Why Gen Z Will Disrupt Multicultural Marketing Models," MediaPost, August 4, 2016, http://www.mediapost.com/publications/ article/280961/3-reasons-gen-z-will-disrupt-multicultural-marketi.html

4   "Multiracial Children," American Academy of Child & Adolescent Psychiatry, April 2016, http://www.aacap.org/aacap/Families_and_Youth/Facts_for_Families/FFF-Guide/Multiracial-Children-071.aspx

5   U.S. Census. "The White Population: 2010" U.S. Census, September 2011, https://www.census.gov/prod/cen2010/briefs/c2010br-05.pdf

6   Chris Hudson, "How Generation Z Are Being Shaped by Technology," UnderstandingTeenagers, http://understandingteenagers.com.au/blog/how-generation-z-are-being-shaped-by-technology/

7   George Beall, "8 Key Differences Between Gen Z and Millennials," Huffington Post, November 5, 2016, http://www.huffingtonpost.com/george-beall/8-key-differences-between_b_12814200.html

8   "Gen Z in the Classroom: Creating the Future," Adobe Educate, October 26, 2016, http://www.adobeeducate.com/genz/adobe-education-genz

9   "Cassandra Report: Gen Z," Deep Focus, April 14, 2015, http://www.deepfocus.net/press/deep-focus-cassandra-report-gen-z-uncovers-massive-attitude-shifts/

10 "The Edge of Seventeen," Cultural Insight, January 6, 2017, http://culturalinsight.com/category/generation-z/

11 Source: Barkley Inc. and FutureCast, LLC., "Getting to Know Gen Z: How the Pivotal Generation is Different from Millennials," 2017.

12 Ryan Scott, "Get Ready for Generation Z," *Forbes*, November 28, 2016, http://www.forbes.com/sites/causeintegration/2016/11/28/get-ready-for-generation-z/#43b12eda1dfe

13 KIDS COUNT Data Book, Annie E. Casey Foundation, 2016, http://www.aecf.org/m/resourcedoc/aecf-the2016kidscountdatabook-2016.pdf

14 Jenn Little, "Generation Z: Who We Are," Voices of Youth, http://www.voicesofyouth.org/en/posts/generation-z--who-we-are

15 Lucy Westcott, "World's Young People Are Most Afraid of Terrorism and Extremism: Report," *Newsweek*, February 8, 2017, http://www.newsweek.com/young-people-terrorism-extremism-fear-generation-z-553839

16 Stefanie O'Connell, "Forget Millennials: 7 Reasons Why Gen Z Is Better with Money," September 19, 2015, https://www.gobankingrates.com/personal-finance/forget-millennials-7-reasons-gen-z-better-money/

17 John Iekel, "Is 'Gen Z' Equipped to Finance Retirement?" ASPPA, November 11, 2016, https://www.asppa.org/News/Article/ArticleID/6958

18 Jeremy Finch, "What is Generation Z, and What Does It Want?" *Fast Company*, May 4, 2015, http://www.fastcoexist.com/3045317/what-is-generation-z-and-what-does-it-want

19 Adapted from the "Gen X vs. Boomer Parenting" chart from "The First Generation of the Twenty-First Century" (2014), by Magid.

20   Source: Barkley Inc. and FutureCast, LLC., "Getting to Know Gen Z: How the Pivotal Generation is Different from Millennials," 2017.

21   "Innovation Imperative: Portrait of Generation Z," Northeastern University 4th Annual Innovation Poll, FTI Consulting, November 18, 2014, http://www.fticonsulting.com/insights/reports/portrait-of-generation-z

22   Shepherd Laughlin, "Gen Z Goes Beyond Gender Binaries in New Innovation Group Data," J. Walter Thompson Intelligence, March 11, 2016, https://www.jwtintelligence.com/2016/03/gen-z-goes-beyond-gender-binaries-in-new-innovation-group-data/

23   Source: Barkley Inc. and FutureCast, LLC., "Getting to Know Gen Z: How the Pivotal Generation is Different from Millennials," 2017.

24   Ibid.

CHAPTER 2

1   "Uniquely Generation Z, What Brands Should Know About Today's Youngest Consumers," 2017 IBM Institute for Business Value Study in collaboration with the National Retail Federation, https://www-01.ibm.com/common/ssi/cgi-bin/ssialias?htmlfid=GBE03799USEN

2   George Beall, "8 Key Differences Between Gen Z and Millennials," Huffington Post, November 5, 2016, http://www.huffingtonpost.com/george-beall/8-key-differences-between_b_12814200.html

3   Gary Vaynerchuk, "This Generation Will Be Fine: Why Social Media Won't Ruin Us," March 16, 2016, https://www.garyvaynerchuk.com/this-generation-will-be-fine-why-social-media-wont-ruin-us/

4   Ibid.

5   Ryan Jenkins, "Generation Z vs. Millennials: The 8 Differences You Need to Know," Inc., July 19, 2017, https://www.inc.com/ryan-jenkins/generation-z-vs-millennials-the-8-differences-you-.html

6   "Uniquely Generation Z: What Brands Should Know About Today's Youngest Consumers." IBM Institute for Business Value in collaboration with the National Retail Federation, January 2017, https://www-935.ibm.com/services/us/gbs/thoughtleadership/uniquelygenz/

7   "Getting to Know Gen Z's Shopping Behaviors," Marketing Charts, July 20, 2016, http://www.marketingcharts.com/traditional/getting-to-know-gen-zs-shopping-behaviors-69200/

8   "Step Aside Millennials: Gen Z Has Arrived," Ideas In Digital, http://www.ideasindigital.com/step-aside-millennials-gen-z-has-arrived/

9   Ibid.

10   "Quizlet.com," Quantcast, https://www.quantcast.com/quizlet.com#/demographics
     Card

11   Lyanne Alfaro, "Your $220 Million to the ALS Ice Bucket Challenge Made a
     Difference, Study Results Show," Business Insider, August 20, 2015, http://
     www.businessinsider.com/your-220-million-to-the-als-bucket-challenge-made-a
     -difference-2015-8

12   "The Gen Z Issue," Cassandra, https://cassandra.co/reports/2015/03/27/gen-z

13   "Marketing to Gen Z Starts by Unlearning Traditional Marketing Principles," Bri-
     an Solis, June 10, 2016, http://www.briansolis.com/2016/06/marketing-generation
     -z-starts-unlearning-traditional-marketing-principles/

14   "Activities of Kids and Teens-US," Mintel Reports, November 2013

15   Amanda Lenhart, "Teens, Technology and Friendships," Pew Research Cen-
     ter, August 6, 2015, http://www.pewinternet.org/2015/08/06/teens-technology
     -and-friendships/

16   Scott Fogel, "Why Everything Brands Say About Gen Z Is Wrong," *Fast Company*,
     October 1, 2015, https://www.fastcocreate.com/3051772/why-everything-brands
     -say-about-gen-z-is-wrong

17   Tessa Wegert, "5 Things Marketers Need to Know About Gen Z," Contently, June
     30, 2016, https://contently.com/strategist/2016/06/30/5-things-marketers-need-to
     -know-gen-z/

18   Source: Barkley Inc. and FutureCast, LLC., "Getting to Know Gen Z: How the
     Pivotal Generation is Different from Millennials," 2017.

19   "Uniquely Generation Z, What Brands Should Know About Today's Youngest
     Consumers," 2017 IBM Institute for Business Value study in collaboration with
     National Retail Federation, https://www-01.ibm.com/common/ssi/cgi-bin/ssialias?
     htmlfid=GBE03799USEN

20   Nicholas Kardaras, "Generation Z: Online and at Risk?" *Scientific American*, Sep-
     tember 1, 2016, https://www.scientificamerican.com/article/generation-z-online
     -and-at-risk/

21   "Gen Z: Get Ready for the Most Self-Conscious, Demanding Consumer Segment,"
     Fung Global Retail & Tech, https://fungglobalretailtech.com/research/gen-z/

22   Connor Blakley, "How to Build a Marketing Campaign That Appeals to Gener-
     ation Z," *Fortune*, December 5, 2016, http://fortune.com/2016/12/05/marketing
     -campaign-generation-z/

23   John Rampton, "7 Ways Marketers Can Reach Gen Z," Entrepreneur, March 10,
     2017, https://www.entrepreneur.com/article/290387

24 "The Everything Guide to Generation Z," Vision Critical, October 2016, https://www.visioncritical.com/wp-content/uploads/2016/10/GenZ_Final.pdf

25 Marion K. Underwood and Robert Faris, "#Being13: Social Media and the Hidden World of Young Adolescents' Peer Culture," 2015, https://www.documentcloud.org/documents/2448422-being-13-report.html

26 Connor Blakley, "How to Build a Marketing Campaign that Appeals to Generation Z," Fortune, December 5, 2016, http://fortune.com/2016/12/05/marketing-campaign-generation-z/

27 "Gen Z Undoes Social Media," SWeb Development, August 24, 2016, http://www.swebdevelopment.com/social-media/gen-z-undoes-social-media/

28 Lauren Johnson, "Taco Bell's Cinco de Mayo Snapchat Lens Was Viewed 224 Million Times," AdWeek, May 11, 2016, http://www.adweek.com/digital/taco-bells-cinco-de-mayo-snapchat-lens-was-viewed-224-million-times-171390/

29 Melanie Shreffler, "Gen Z Is Already Misunderstood," MediaPost, October 15, 2015, http://www.mediapost.com/publications/article/260463/gen-z-is-already-misunderstood.html

30 Suzanne Bearne, "Forget Millennials, Brands Need to Win over Generation Z," May 22, 2015, http://www.campaignlive.co.uk/article/forget-millennials-brands-need-win-generation-z/1348169#YJDeeSyBk0KowSfd.99

CHAPTER 3

1 "Step Aside, Millennials: Gen Z Has Arrived," Ideas In Digital, http://www.ideasindigital.com/step-aside-millennials-gen-z-has-arrived/

2 "Gen Z: A Look Inside Its Mobile-First Mindset," Think with Google, https://www.thinkwithgoogle.com/interactive-report/gen-z-a-look-inside-its-mobile-first-mindset

3 "Mobile and Tablet Internet Usage Exceeds Desktop for the First Time Worldwide," StatCounter, November 1, 2016, http://gs.statcounter.com/press/mobile-and-tablet-internet-usage-exceeds-desktop-for-first-time-worldwide

4 PepsiCo, "Chasing Exhilaration, Mountain Dew® Captures the Euphoric Feeling of Doing with New Global Campaign," PR Newswire, January 9, 2017, http://www.prnewswire.com/news-releases/chasing-exhilaration-mountain-dew-captures-the-euphoric-feeling-of-doing-with-new-global-campaign-300387602.html

5 Alex Williams, "Move over, Millennials, Here Comes Generation Z," New York Times, September 18, 2015, https://www.nytimes.com/2015/09/20/fashion/move-over-millennials-here-comes-generation-z.html?_r=0

6 Meg Cannistra, "4 Great Examples of Satisfying Snackable content," Ceros, April 13, 2016, https://www.ceros.com/blog/4-great-examples-of-snackable-content/

7   Kevin McSpadden, "You Now Have a Shorter Attention Span Than a Goldfish," *Time*, May 14, 2015, http://time.com/3858309/attention-spans-goldfish/

8   "'Gen Z': The Next Generation of Foodies," *Food Business News*, November 9, 2015, http://www.foodbusinessnews.net/articles/news_home/Consumer_Trends/2015/11/Gen_Z_the_next_generation_of_f.aspx?ID=%7BFC837626-9EF0-4E9B-95E6-308B162072BA%7D&cck=1

9   Lauren Johnson, "How Tasty's Addictive Cooking Videos Helped Buzzfeed Build a Food Empire," *AdWeek*, October 30, 2016, http://www.adweek.com/digital/how-tasty-mastered-social-publishing-part-buzzfeed-s-plan-make-50-revenue-video-174325/

10 Marina Lopes, "Videos may make up 84 percent of internet traffic by 2018: Cisco," Reuters, June 10, 2014, http://www.reuters.com/article/us-internet-consumers-cisco-systems/videos-may-make-up-84-percent-of-internet-traffic-by-2018-cisco-idUSKBN0EL15E20140610

11 Allison Boatman, "4 Reasons Why Visual Communication Has a Big Impact," TechSmith, January 31, 2017, https://blogs.techsmith.com/tips-how-tos/why-visual-communication-matters/

12 Karla Gutierrez, "Studies Confirm the Power of Visuals in eLearning," Shift, July 8, 2014, http://info.shiftelearning.com/blog/bid/350326/Studies-Confirm-the-Power-of-Visuals-in-eLearning

13 Haig Kouyoumdijan, "Learning Through Visuals," *Psychology Today*, July 20, 2012, https://www.psychologytoday.com/blog/get-psyched/201207/learning-through-visuals

14 "Gen Z Video Viewing Is Increasingly Social, but YouTube Still Rules This Sector—While TV Falls Further Behind," Business Wire, March 31, 2016, https://www.bulldogreporter.com/gen-z-video-viewing-is-increasingly-social-but-youtube-still-rules-this-sector-while-tv-falls-further-behind/

15 "Generation Z Loves Mobile Video—Just Don't Tell Them to Watch It," Marketing Communication News, August 31, 2016, http://www.thedrum.com/news/2016/08/31/gen-z-loves-mobile-video-just-don-t-tell-them-watch-it

16 Ibid.

17 Ibid.

18 "Brands Get Ready—Gen Z Are Growing Up and Ready to Challenge Says Kantar Millward Brown," Kantar Millward Brown, January 10, 2017, http://www.millwardbrown.com/global-navigation/news/press-releases/full-release/2017/01/10/brands-get-ready---gen-z-are-growing-up-and-ready-to-challenge-says-kantar-millward-brown

19 Meg Cannistra, "4 Great Examples of Satisfying Snackable Content," Ceros Blog, April 13, 2016, https://www.ceros.com/blog/4-great-examples-of-snackable-content/

20   "3 Tips for Re-Thinking Your Culture of Content and Engagement to Reach Gen Z,"
      2017, http://www.millennialmarketing.com/2017/05/3-tips-for-re-thinking-your
      -culture-of-content-and-engagement-to-reach-gen-z/

21   Tessa Wegert, "5 Things Marketers Need to Know About Gen Z," June 30, 2016,
      Contently, https://contently.com/strategist/2016/06/30/5-things-marketers-need
      -to-know-gen-z/

22   "AdReaction: Engaging Gen X, Y and Z," Kantar Millward Brown, http://www.
      millwardbrown.com/adreaction/genxyz/us/what-people-think-about-advertising/
      preferred-video-ad-formats

23   "Getting Gen Z Primed to Save the World," The Atlantic, sponsored content, All-
      state, http://www.theatlantic.com/sponsored/allstate/getting-gen-z-primed-to-save
      -the-world/747/

24   Rick Wartzman, "Coming Soon to Your Office: Gen Z," Time, February 12, 2014,
      http://time.com/6693/coming-soon-to-your-office-gen-z/

25   "Donate Cell Phones to a Good Cause with the Help of HopeLine," Verizon
      Wireless, October 1, 2014, https://www.verizonwireless.com/articles/donate-cell
      -phones-to-a-good-cause-with-the-help-of-hopeline/?intcmp=vzwdom

CHAPTER 4

1   Molly Thompson, "Description of How Marketers Can Use Maslow's Hierar-
      chy of Needs," http://smallbusiness.chron.com/description-marketers-can-use
      -maslows-hierarchy-needs-39333.html

2   "Zeno Group Releases the Human Project 2016," Press Release, March 2, 2016,
      https://www.zenogroup.com/zeno-group-releases-the-human-project-2016/

3   George Carey, TEDxNaperville, https://www.youtube.com/watch?v=yLir3pHD3kI

4   Jens Manuel Krogstad, "5 Facts About the Modern American Family," Factank,
      April 30, 2014, http://www.pewresearch.org/fact-tank/2014/04/30/5-facts-about
      -the-modern-american-family/

5   "Children Have Refined Pester Power and Make Savvy Shoppers," YouGov Om-
      nibus Research, June 11, 2015, https://today.yougov.com/news/2015/06/11/
      children-make-savvy-shoppers-have-refined-pester-p/

6   All figures in the chart are from YouGov Plc. Total sample size was 1,057 adults. Field-
      work was undertaken between March 4–13, 2015. The survey was carried out online.
      The figures have been weighted and are representative of all US adults (aged 18+).

7   Albert Caruana and Rosella Vassallo, "Children's Perception of Their Influence over
      Purchases: The Role of Parental Communication Patterns," *Journal of Consumer
      Marketing*, February 2003, https://www.researchgate.net/publication/247615154_
      Children%27s_perception_of_their_influence_over_purchases_The_role_of_
      parental_communication_patterns

8 C+R Research/YouthBeat Total Year 2016 data

9 "Generation Z Is the Driving Influence on New Customer Spending Patterns," HRC Retail Advisory, 2016, http://hrcadvisory.com/wp-content/uploads/2016/11/HRC-Consumer-Shopping-Survey_Key-Findings.pdf

10 Lauren E. Sherman, Ashley A. Payton, Leanna M. Hernandez, Patricia M. Greenfield, and Mirella Dapretto, "The Power of the *Like* in Adolescence," *Psychological Science*, Vol. 27, No. 7, 2016, http://journals.sagepub.com/doi/abs/10.1177/0956797616645673

11 Stuart Wolpert, "The Teenage Brain on Social Media," UCLA Newsroom, May 31, 2016, http://newsroom.ucla.edu/releases/the-teenage-brain-on-social-media

12 "10 Reasons Why Influencer Marketing Is the Next Big Thing," *AdWeek*, July 14, 2015, http://www.adweek.com/digital/10-reasons-why-influencer-marketing-is-the-next-big-thing/

13 Tapinfluence, https://www.tapinfluence.com/

14 "Deep Focus' Cassandra Report: Gen Z Uncovers Massive Attitude Shifts Toward Money, Work and Communication Preferences," Market Wired, March 30, 2015, http://www.marketwired.com/press-release/deep-focus-cassandra-report-gen-z-uncovers-massive-attitude-shifts-toward-money-work-2004889.htm

15 Susanne Ault, "Digital Star Popularity Grows Versus Mainstream Celebrities," *Variety*, July 23, 2015, http://variety.com/2015/digital/news/youtubers-teen-survey-ksi-pewdiepie-1201544882/

16 Celie O'Neill-Hart and Howard Blumenstein, "Why YouTube Stars Are More Influential Than Traditional Celebrities," Think with Google, July 2016, https://www.thinkwithgoogle.com/infographics/youtube-stars-influence.html

17 Jessica Liu, "Category Influencer Programs Are the New Paid Endorsements," Forrester, January 6, 2017, https://www.forrester.com/report/Category+Influencer+Programs+Are+The+New+Paid+Endorsements/-/E-RES136627

18 Joseph Steinberg, "10 Tips for Working with Social Media Influencers," *Inc.*, April 17, 2016, https://www.inc.com/joseph-steinberg/10-tips-for-working-with-social-media-influencers.html

19 Ibid.

20 Ibid.

CHAPTER 5

1 Kristie Wong, "Generation Z—Who Are They?" December 15, 2016, http://blog.btrax.com/en/2016/12/15/generation-z-who-are-they/

2 Source: Barkley Inc. and FutureCast, LLC., "Getting to Know Gen Z: How the Pivotal Generation is Different from Millennials," 2017.

3   "How Social Media Dictates Happiness for Generations After Millennials: Gen Z," The Center for Generational Kinetics, February 1, 2016, http://genhq.com/how-social-media-dictates-happiness-for-generations-after-millennials/

4   "Children, Teens, Media, and Body Image," Common Sense Media, January 21, 2015, https://www.commonsensemedia.org/research/children-teens-media-and-body-image

5   Nick Reggars and Kirby Todd, "Social Habits of Highly Effective Teens," Medium, May 21, 2015, https://medium.com/@sfheat/social-habits-of-highly-effective-teens-af45d60f5e06

6   Deborah Weinswig, "Deep Dive: Gen Z and Beauty—The Social Media Symbiosis," Fung Global Retail and Technology, February 27, 2017, https://www.fungglobalretailtech.com/research/deep-dive-gen-z-beauty-social-media-symbiosis/

7   Ibid.

8   Kate Dwyer, "Why Some of Biggest Stars Are Deleting Their Accounts—And Maybe You Should, Too," Teen Vogue, October 14, 2015, https://www.teenvogue.com/story/generation-z-teens-ditch-social-media

9   "Your Teen's Personal Online Brand," *Family Circle*, September 30, 2013, http://www.familycircle.com/blogs/momster/2013/09/30/your-teens-personal-brand/

10 Nicholas Kardaras, "Generation Z: Online and at Risk?" *Scientific American*, September 1, 2016, https://www.scientificamerican.com/article/generation-z-online-and-at-risk/

11 Emma Ryan, "A Guide For Marketing to Generation Z: Be Blunt, Be Engaging + Be Trustworthy," Wilde Agency, August 11, 2016, http://www.wildeagency.com/guide-to-marketing-to-generation-z/

12 Mark Schaefer, "Why Customer Personas May Be an Outdated Marketing Technique," April 27, 2015, Business Grow, https://www.businessesgrow.com/2015/04/27/customer-personas/

13 Abercrombie & Fitch, "2016 Annual Investor Report," http://ir.abercrombie.com/anf/investors/investorrelations.html

14 Monica Sarkar, "H&M's Latest Look: Hijab-Wearing Muslim Model Stirs Debate," CNN, August 26, 2016, http://www.cnn.com/2015/09/29/europe/hm-hijab-model/index.html

15 John Kell, "Majority of Nike's U.S. Employees Are Minorities for the First Time," *Fortune*, May 12, 2016, http://fortune.com/2016/05/12/nike-staff-diversity/

16 Victor De Vita, "Creating Brand Desire: Finding the Generation Z 'Sweet Spot,'" *Forbes*, June 8, 2017, https://www.forbes.com/sites/forbescommunicationscouncil/2017/06/08/creating-brand-desire-finding-the-generation-z-sweet-spot/#5d631799713e

17 Katie Carlson, "The Psychology of Brand Trust and Influencer Marketing," Experticity, February 2, 2016, https://business.experticity.com/the-psychology-of-brand-trust-influencer-marketing/

18   "Do Emotions Sell?" Marketing Enhancement Group, Inc., http://www.meg
      -research.com/downloads/Do-Emotions-Sell.pdf

CHAPTER 6

1   Anjali Lai, The Rise of the Empowered Customer: Consumers' Evolving Behaviors
      and Attitudes Set the Pace for Innovation," Forrester, July 12, 2016, https://www.
      forrester.com/report/The+Rise+Of+The+Empowered+Customer/-/E-RES133207

2   "What Is Your State of Credit?" Experian, 2016, http://www.experian.com/live
      -credit-smart/state-of-credit-2016.html

3   Shannon Insler, "5 Important Money Lessons You Can Learn from Gen Z," Stu-
      dent Loan Hero, February 14, 2017, https://studentloanhero.com/featured/gen-z
      -5-important-money-lessons/

4   "Uniquely Generation Z: What Brands Should Know About Today's Young-
      est Consumers," IBM Institute for Business Value in collaboration with Nation-
      al Retail Federation, January 2017, https://www-935.ibm.com/services/us/gbs/
      thoughtleadership/uniquelygenz/

5   Amanda Lenhart, "Teens, Social Media & Technology Overview 2015," Pew Re-
      search Center, April 9, 2015, http://www.pewinternet.org/2015/04/09/teens
      -social-media-technology-2015/

6   "Gen Z and the Future of Retail," Fitch, http://www.fitch.com/think/gen-z-and
      -the-future-of-retail

7   Adapted from original source: Fitch, "Gen Z and the Future of Retail," 2017.

8   Ibid.

9   Maria Bobila, "Generation Z: A Primer on Their Shopping and Fashion Hab-
      its," Fashionista, January 27, 2017, https://fashionista.com/2017/01/generation-z
      -shopping-habits

10   Original source: Euclid, Inc., Evolution of Retail: Gen Z Shopper Report, March
      17.

11   "Generation Z Is the Driving Influence on New Customer Spending Patterns," HRC
      Retail Advisory, Fall 2016, http://hrcadvisory.com/wp-content/uploads/2016/11/
      HRC-Consumer-Shopping-Survey_Key-Findings.pdf

12   Max Berlinger, "Teenage Dream: How Urban Outfitters Is Navigating a Rocky Retail
      Scene," Refinery29, April 19, 2017, http://www.refinery29.com/2017/04/149086/
      urban-outfitters-teen-shopping-trends

13   Vivian Hendriksz, "Urban Outfitters: 'Every Store Is like an Experiment,'" Fashion
      United, September 4, 2015, https://fashionunited.com/news/retail/urban-outfitters
      -every-store-is-like-an-experiment/201509048078

14 Daphne Howland, "How Generation Z Is Transforming the Shopping Experience," RetailDive, March 29, 2017, http://www.retaildive.com/news/how-generation -z-is-transforming-the-shopping-experience/438194/

15 "Despite Living a Digital Life, 98 Percent of Generation Z Still Shop In-Store," Joint Press Release: IBM and NRF, January 12, 2017, https://nrf.com/media/ press-releases/despite-living-digital-life-98-percent-of-generation-z-still-shop-store

16 "Uniquely Generation Z: What Brands Should Know About Today's Youngest Consumers." IBM Institute for Business Value in collaboration with National Retail Federation, January 2017, https://www-935.ibm.com/services/us/gbs/ thoughtleadership/uniquelygenz/

17 Content Square, "Generation Z Market Study," 2017, http://go.contentsquare. com/hubfs/eBooks/%5BeBook%5D%20Generation%20Z%20%7C%20 ContentSquare.pdf?t=1501076556347

18 Carl Hartmann, "3 Tips for Pleasing the Demanding Gen Z Online Shopper," Digital Commerce 360, December 6, 2016, https://www.digitalcommerce360 .com/2016/12/06/3-tips-pleasing-demanding-gen-z-online-shopper/

CHAPTER 7

1 Jeff Bezos, "Online Extra: Jeff Bezos on Word-of-Mouth Power," Bloomberg, August 1, 2004, https://www.bloomberg.com/news/articles/2004-08-01/online-extra -jeff-bezos-on-word-of-mouth-power

2 "Raising The Bar: How Generations Are Reshaping Brand Experiences," a Custom Technology Adoption Profile commissioned by American Express, May 2017, http://about.americanexpress.com/news/docs/Amex-Forrester-Gen-Z-Research. pdf

3 Leonie Roderick, "Why brand purpose requires more than just a snappy slogan," Marketing Week, February 15, 2016, https://www.marketingweek. com/2016/02/15/why-brands-must-prove-their-purpose-beyond-profit/

4 Natalia Angulo, "77% of Gen Z consumers want brands to reach out: Survey," Marketing Dive, Feb. 16, 2016, https://www.marketingdive.com/news/77-of-gen -z-consumers-want-brands-to-reach-out-survey/413887/

5 Generation Z to Switch the Majority of Purchases to Retailers that Provide the Newest Digital Tools and Channels, Accenture Global Consumer Shopping Survey 2017, https://www.accenture.com/t20170210T012359__w__/us-en/_acnmedia/ PDF-44/Accenture-Retail-Customer-Journey-Research-2017-Infographic.pdf

6 "The Next Generation of Retail," Retail Perceptions, July 2016, http://www. retailperceptions.com/2016/07/the-next-generation-of-retail/

7 Chantal Fernandez, "Inside Lululemon's Unconventional Influencer Network," Fashionista, November 2, 2016, http://fashionista.com/2016/11/lululemon-ambassadors

8   Ashley Rodriguez, "Stung by Millennial Misses, Brands Retool for Gen Z," *Ad-Age*, May 19, 2015, http://adage.com/article/cmo-strategy/informed-millennial -misses-brands-retool-gen-z/298641/

9   Daphne Howland, "Target Gets Creative Help from Gen Z in New Apparel Line," Retail Dive, January 12, 2017, http://www.retaildive.com/news/target-gets -creative-help-from-gen-z-in-new-apparel-line/433922/

10 Bea McMonagle, "Members of Target's Retail Collaboration—Class of 2017—Chat Generation Z's Shopping Habits," *Forbes*, March 15, 2017, https://www.forbes .com/sites/beamcmonagle/2017/03/15/members-of-targets-retail-collaboration -class-of-2017-chat-generation-zs-shopping-habits/#74c33ea06067

11 Sam Frizell, "6 Things to Know About Apple CEO Tim Cook," Time, Oct. 30, 2014, http://time.com/3548342/tim-cook-apple/

12 "Netflix and Chill," according to UrbanDictionary.com, is "the new way of inviting your partner over to be together alone, but both of you know, although you might not say it, what it will lead to. Hence, the term can now be used in place of the word "sex."

13 "Piper Jaffray 32nd Semi-Annual Taking Stock with Teens Survey," BusinessWire, Fall 2016, http://mms.businesswire.com/media/20161014005550/en/549773/5/ Combined_Infographic_-_JPEG.jpg?download=1

14 Rakin Azfar, "Sephora Promotes Nationwide Social Impact Initiative Through Mobile Channels," Mobile Marketer, http://www.mobilemarketer.com/ex/mobilemarketer/ cms/news/social-networks/23708.html

15 Hayley Peterson, "It Costs Nearly Nothing to Open a Chick-Fil-A—but There's a Catch," Business Insider, April 22, 2017, http://www.businessinsider.com/what-it -costs-to-open-a-chick-fil-a-2017-4

16 Clark Schultz, "Chick-Fil-A Continues to Gobble Up Market Share," Seeking Alpha, July 11, 2016, https://seekingalpha.com/news/3192530-chick-fil-continues -gobble-market-share

17 Hayley Peterson, "Chick-fil-A Is Making Big Changes to Take on Shake Shack and Chipotle," Business Insider, March 21, 2016, http://www.businessinsider.com/ chick-fil-a-is-reinventing-itself-2016-3

18 Thomas Koulopoulos, "Watch Heineken School Pepsi on How to Advertise to Gen Z (It's a Lesson for Every Brand)," *Inc.*, April 27, 2017, https://www.inc.com/thom-as-koulopoulos/watch-heineken-school-pepsi-on-how-to-advertise-to-gen-z-its-a -lesson-for-every-.html

19 "Reaching Generation Z with Experiential Marketing," The Pineapple Agency, http://thepineappleagency.com/experiential-marketing/reaching-generation-z-with -experiential-marketing/

20 "Marketing to the iGeneration," Mintel, US, April 2016, http://reports.mintel .com/display/748696/

21 Ibid.

22 Nicholas Brown, "Generation Z and the Future of Print Marketing," Business.com, February 22, 2017, https://www.business.com/articles/nicholas-brown-generation -z-and-the-future-of-print-marketing/

23 Roy Eduardo Kokoyachuk, "ThinkNow Gen™ We Are Gen Z: We Are Shoppers Report," ThinkNow Research, February 1, 2017, http://www.thinknowresearch. com/blog/thinknow-gen-we-are-gen-z-we-are-shoppers-report/

CHAPTER 8

1 Susan Wojcicki, "The Eight Pillars of Innovation," Think with Google, July 2011, https://www.thinkwithgoogle.com/marketing-resources/8-pillars-of-innovation/

2 Jack Myers, "Who are Gen Z and Why Do You Need to Meet Them?" MediaVillage, February 21, 2017, https://www.mediavillage.com/article/who-are-gen-z-and -why-do-you-need-to-meet-them/

3 John Zogby, "Millennials on the Move: How Communities Can Retain Them," *Forbes*, June 20, 2017, https://www.forbes.com/sites/johnzogby/2017/06/20/ millennials-on-the-move-how-communities-can-retain-them/#1f702da03944

4 Katherine Barrett and Richard Greene, "Generation Z Wants a Job. Are You Ready to Hire Them?," Governing the States and Localities; March 23, 2017, http://www. governing.com/columns/smart-mgmt/gov-generation-z-workforce.html

5 Conscious Capitalism, n.d., https://www.consciouscapitalism.org/

INDEX